A BRIEF HISTORY OF SOCCER

FROM VICTORIAN BRITAIN TO A GLOBAL PHENOMENON

PAUL FRENCH

UNBEATABLE OFFER

At the back of this book, you'll find an *unbeatable* offer as my thank you to you. Don't forget to check it out.

Old Carthusians 2007-2012
SFC Friedrichshain Internazionale 2014-2018

Thanks for the memories

"I didn't do it because I wanted to write history. I did it because I wanted to give 90 minutes of joy to people."

— ARRIGO SACCHI

Football vs. Soccer

In most places where the word *football* would normally be used, including some direct quotations, it has been replaced with the word *soccer.*

This will please some and horrify others.

1. INTRODUCTION

On the pitch, you see good ideas all the time. I play for an international team in Berlin made up of players from 14 different countries. We have an American in the squad, the California kid, Andy Liu. As a player, Andy is so elusive that we have dubbed him 'Luiesta' because his style resembles that strange Spanish phantom, Andres Iniesta.

One day, I noticed that Andy and I had very different reference points as a fan. He loves playing the game, but I couldn't exchange notes with him about watching Des Lynam's mustache on 1990s *Match of the Day*. James Richardson mainlining macchiatos and blowing *buongiornos* into British living rooms on Sunday mornings? Not part of his childhood. Or yours, I wager. So an idea began to take hold.

I wondered about being a fan of the game growing up in America, and if there was place for a crash course in soccer history. My hunch was that most Americans did not want to read a 600-page tome. But they might like the extended highlights. I had read Jonathan Wilson's *Inverting the Pyramid* (and will happily box anyone who doesn't consider this the best book ever written about soccer), but knew that this wasn't quite the right tool for the job.

In the spring of 2015, my drooling appreciation for one of this universe's own prototypes, Lionel Messi, led me to compare two separate online reports of one of the 700-and-something goals he has scored so far.

The first, from British journalist Sid Lowe in *The Guardian*:

"Messi was magnificent and scored twice, the first after 20 minutes was the goal that set up this victory and one that even he will surely consider extraordinary. A moment before, he had confronted Mikel Balenziaga, who had been pulling at his shirt. Now, revenge was exacted. He confronted the defender again, with the ball this time. Messi received possession on the right touchline, rolled the ball under his foot and set off. Balenziaga and Beñat Etxebarria were left behind, Balenziaga twice. Mikel Rico was next, then Ameyric Laporte. Cutting into the area, Messi hit the ball hard and low into the net at the near post.

"Iago Herrerín wore specially designed commemorative gloves for this final, embossed with the names of every goalkeeper who had played a Cup final for Athletic. He could not reach it; none of them would have been able to. All around the stadium, hands held heads in disbelief, a simple question repeated over and over: *how?* 'I still don't know the full magnitude of the goal, because I was alongside him on the touchline,' Luis Enrique said. 'I'm looking forward to being able to enjoy it on the television.'

"It was one of those moments that leaves you as helpless and baffled as the defenders wondering what had just happened, equally incapable of explaining it. How to describe *that*? How to do it justice? "Don't write about Messi, watch him," Pep Guardiola once said. A picture paints a thousand words, after all. This picture painted a hundred thousand words and all of them were superlatives. It was a ridiculous goal, one that had a stupefying effect on this stadium."

Then the second, from a video report on ESPN:

"During the 2015 Copa del Rey final, Lionel Messi demonstrated the skills that make him the best footballer on the planet with his first goal of the match. After receiving the ball just past midfield, Messi goes from virtually 0 to 19.5mph in just 2.7 seconds. That's an acceleration on par with an American Football speedster, NFL All-Pro Jamaal Charles. And Messi does it with the ball at his feet. But as three defenders trap him on the sideline, each coming within 6 feet of the ball, Messi begins to decelerate. This allows him to make three short controlled touches, effectively beating the Bilbao players in just 1.2 seconds. As he enters the box, Messi uses an inside-out move to open up more than five feet of space. This gives him just enough room to rip a 48mph near-post shot that misses the keeper's outstretched hand by less than six inches.

"In a span of just over 11 seconds, in a possession that covered nearly 60 yards, the ball was more than 2 feet away from Messi just twice and for a grand total of less than 2 seconds. And the finish was just as spectacular as the dribble. To fit the ball in a window that small from 14 yards away, Messi's lateral aim couldn't be off by more than 0.75 of a single degree. That means if Messi's point of contact on the ball shifted left or right by just 1.5 mm, he misses. That's a margin of error about the width of a blade of grass. And the incredible precision Messi showed on this goal is why in La Liga this season, Messi converted on his shots at a rate 21% higher than the average forward. For ESPN Sport Science, I'm John Brenkus."

These two reports were so different that I decided to offer my own bridge between two spectator cultures. So here it is, a crash course in soccer, from the keyboard of a Brit to the Kindle of a Yank. It is designed to take only as long to read as it does to watch a game of soccer. In 105 minutes (90 mins + 15 for half-time), you can whizz through soccer's kaleidoscopic highlights package and come to know more about the game than 98% of your friends.

And 99% of all Englishmen.

Straight In,
    Paul French

Palm Springs, California, April 2017

2. CREATION

"A man who dares to waste one hour of time has not discovered the value of life."
~ CHARLES DARWIN

"Everything I know about morality and the obligations of men, I owe it to soccer."
~ ALBERT CAMUS

S occer is about 150 years old. There are plenty of myths about its beginnings, from ancient Greece to Kamakura Japan to the beaches of the Caribbean, but the game as we know it today was forged in Victorian Britain, around the same time that John D. Rockefeller incorporated Standard Oil and Major League Baseball began. The exact dates are fuzzy (like the offside rule), but 150 is an easy number to remember. If you picture steel wires hoisting a giant, neon '150' sign onto the side of the newly-constructed Brooklyn Bridge, you'll never forget how old soccer is.

The origin story is both brutal and romantic, as opposed to just obscene, which is one way to describe entire towns kicking a pig's bladder from one landmark to the other in 9th Century England. One thousand years later, it was played in the green fields and stone cloisters of grandiose private schools like Charterhouse, Eton, and Westminster, which are known as public schools in Britain because they are open to the paying public. In the early days, different schools played different versions and the game was all about dribbling. There was no passing or even defending. The number of players was already settled, but these eleven just ran after the ball, waiting for their own precious chance to run the gauntlet until they were enthusiastically slaughtered.

Despite the civilized backdrop, few activities except for actual war could have been more barbaric. Hacking opponents' shins until they stumbled and fell was a celebrated skill that would become a bone of contention between those holding different visions of the game. So too would picking the ball up and running with it. Attempting this in a professional league today is called rugby, but in soccer, it would result in ridicule, and a lengthy ban. For the masters watching from the sidelines, soccer was the perfect physical antidote to moral turpitude and the decline of the Empire. Or so they thought. On the pitch it was a different story - this was no place for old liberals or young fools. In fact, the spectacle of early soccer was very similar to what happens when you let children chase a ball around a playground unsupervised: they become beasts. It was savage, unruly, often unfair and sometimes banned. In his book *From Cloisters to Cup Finals: A History of Charterhouse Football,* Malcolm Bailey writes, "As Dickens advised in his novels, the schools needed to fight back and education became revolutionized, as did the art of soccer. The game that had been regarded by many as plebeian was civilized by the public schools." Nevertheless, war was - and remains - a very robust metaphor for soccer, with lines of players who have specific roles. Professor Francisco Vargas, who has a long-standing relationship with FC Barcelona, observes that the game "has evolved in these four areas: defend, construct, rebuild, besiege."

To the likes of Great Britain, France and Russia, who were in the great global power club at the time of soccer's birth, the United States ranked in importance diplomatically, militarily and politically with the likes of, say, Belgium. Historians have dubbed the 20th Century The American Century and yet that is an outcome that few people saw coming. Records show a weak navy and a small army. It was able to field major military formations if it had to, but the U.S. was a country that had recently had its biggest ever war not in a bold and adventurous crusade, but against itself. Soccer was not on the menu yet. Meanwhile, the British public schools were squabbling over what the rules should be, how they should be decided and who got to make the decision. In hindsight though, this debate was legitimate. It took awhile for soccer and rugby to officially fork (and rugby itself later forked between rugby union and rugby league), but the separate games are still being played today, so you can say that both camps had a good case.

If you visit London and make your way to Covent Garden, you can visit the pub where the separation agreement was reached. If you're not in a hurry, do also pause and take in the architecture of Inigo Jones' Vitruvian Tuscan church. On 8 December 1863, at the Freemason's Tavern, 81-82 Long Acre, it was decreed that two separate winter sports were required to satisfy the appetites of Britain's 19th Century schoolboys. Interestingly, the main topic of debate was not whether or not players should be allowed to use their hands, but whether aiming kicks at opponents' shin bones should be allowed. One man, F.W. Campbell of Blackheath, was so adamant that hacking was key to the spirit of the game that he resigned from the football association when it was banned. Any Englishman who's watched the national team's last fifteen tournaments might wonder if the country will ever be rid of this impressively regressive bulldog DNA.

That dribbling survived long enough for Lionel Messi to launch his ludicrous 2015 assault on the Bilbao defence is thanks mainly to Law Six, the prototype of the offside rule: "When a player has kicked the ball, anyone of the same side who is nearer the opponent's goal-line is out of play..." So players had to either pass backwards or sideways. If they wanted to move the ball up the pitch, it would have to remain at their feet. This changed in 1866, when an exception was made - forward passes would be allowed as long as there were at least three members of the other team between the player and the opponent's goal when the ball was played. It stayed like this for the next 70 years.

Just three weeks before the meeting took place at Freemason's Tavern in London, Abraham Lincoln had issued the foundation stone of American history, the Gettysburg address, in Pennsylvania. He determined that "all men are created equal" and insisted that a "government of the people, for the people, shall not perish from this earth." He didn't go so far as to outlaw hacking, but it was a bedrock of simple, powerful truths. Soccer may have been shepherded into officialdom by the British elite, but over the next hundred years it would shed some dogmas of the past and develop a calling to bring freedom, opportunity and joy to citizens all over the world.

3. THE GRADUATE

"He would get you doing step-overs, little turns and twist on the ball and everything you did was to make you comfortable on the ball."
~ BIG RON ATKINSON on Jimmy Hogan

"Mrs Robinson, you're trying to seduce me, aren't you?"
~ BENJAMIN, *The Graduate*

Slowly, formations started to appear to add some symmetry to the mindless kick and rush. 1-2-7 and 2-2-6 were the early favorites. In 1872, soccer's first international match took place, between England and Scotland. It ended 0-0, but was historic because for the first time observers noticed different styles and reported their findings. England were bigger, stronger and extremely direct, while Scotland were lighter in physique and passed the ball between themselves on the way up the pitch. This was new.

1872 was the same year that the first FA Cup was held. 2,000 people watched the final at the Kennington Oval Cricket Ground in South London as Wanderers beat Royal Engineers 1-0. Today, Kennington is in the middle of one of London's great regeneration projects, with the new American Embassy making its home down the road on Nine Elms Lane. Back then, it was an over-populated place of ill-repute and a breeding ground for diphtheria. Just fifteen of the Football Association's 50 registered teams entered (and three withdrew without playing a game), but for the goalscorer Morton Betts, the honor of scoring the inaugural trophy-winning goal in the longest-standing club competition in the world remains. It was a tap-in.

At the turn of the century, some teams started experimenting with a 2-3-5 formation and cooperation between teammates gradually forced its way into the collective consciousness. Goalkeepers were given a different colored shirt in 1909, and asked to stay inside their own special box a couple of years later. Progress, you can see, was slow. But mass marketing was not. Everywhere the British went, they took soccer. Countless trade and commerce missions planted football in South America. In Europe, to visit a sports club in the late 19th Century was to witness an unironic admiration of Victorian England. You can google the photos to admire the coy looks, twirly moustaches and, in some places, long cotton trousers where you would expect to see shorts.

Once it was agreed that passing was the way forward, the ramshackle beginnings of soccer dissolved into a relatively stable period and 2-3-5 became the de facto global formation. Astonishingly, not much changed before the First World War. This seems hard to believe, but while there was certainly increased interest in different playing styles, formational experimentation as we know it today was limited.

After things calmed down on the Western front, the tactical chatter picked up again, most notably in the coffee houses of central and eastern Europe. The lives of two men, one English and one Austrian, heralded a significant change in the way people thought about soccer. When people talk about the great coaches of the world, their time frame is often restricted to television footage and perhaps to the memories of their fathers. But you can tell anyone who tells you that Sir Alex Ferguson or Pep Guardiola have no equal that they've forgotten about Englishman James "Jimmy" Hogan, who was born in 1882.

When his playing career stuttered over a knee injury aged twenty-eight, Hogan took a coaching role in Holland with Dordrecht, where he began to put into practice the coaching methods he believed should have existed when he was a player. He focused on ball control, tactics and positioning and drew the admiration of the second most important coach most people have not heard of, the great father of Austrian football, Hugo Meisl.

Like Hogan, Meisl had not been a spectacular player. Following the wishes of a middle-class Jewish family, he went into banking. He kept one foot in the game, also working for the Austrian Football Federation until one day, he found himself in charge of things and dropped the banking. Meisl appointed Hogan on a combination of a friend's advice and his own intuition, hoping that he would also be useful offering coaching advice to the top Austrian clubs.

The two put their heads together to prepare the Austrian national squad for the 1912 Stockholm Olympics, losing 4-3 to Holland in the quarter finals. Meisl was sufficiently convinced by Hogan to give him the job full time, with a focus on the 1916 Berlin Olympics. War got in the way (the games never took place), and Hogan, stranded in Austria while his wife and children returned safely to Britain, ended up traveling east to coach Budapest club MTK. He was successful, bringing MTK the title in 1916-17. Hogan returned to Britain as soon as the war ended, but MTK hung to the title for nine consecutive years.

Meanwhile, Meisl took Hogan's philosophies and started laying the groundwork for soccer's first legendary side, the Wunderteam. In the Danubian school, as it was known, technique took centre stage. From a distance, this does not differ so much from the observation that English physicality was inferior to the Scottish passing game, but it was symptomatic of a larger trend. In South America, technique also came first, individuality a very close second. 'Game after game,' wrote the great Uruguayan journalist Eduardo Galeano in Soccer in Sun and Shadow, 'the crowd jostled to see those men, slippery as squirrels, who played chess with the ball. The English squad had perfected the long pass and the high ball, but these disinherited children from far-off Argentina didn't walk in their father's footsteps. They chose to invent a game of close passes directly to the foot, with lightning changes in rhythm and high-speed dribbling.'

The first major tactical shift in soccer took place in 1925, ironically enough the same year that the teaching of evolution was prohibited by the Butler Act in the state of Tennessee. Thankfully it is more straightforward to confirm a factual account of the origin of the offside law than to deny the Biblical account of man's origin. As we know, the existing offside law stated that three opposing players had to be between an attacking player and his opponent's goal. The problem was that teams had taken to playing with one deep-lying defender while the rest of the team pushed up twenty yards. Games become boring.

One proposal by the FA was to install a line in each half 40 yards (37 meters) from goal. If a forward was behind this line, it was suggested, he could not be offside. But the more elegant solution was to simply change the rule to "two opponents". Goals per game skyrocketed. Records show a 35% increase in goals in the Football League from the 1924-25 season and the rule change was approved by the International Board before the following season.

By most measures this adjustment had been a success, but in history as in physics, every action has an equal and opposite. This was the tipping point for 2-3-5, as the 'third back' emerged to combat the expanded space the forwards now had to operate in. The idea to turn 2-3-5 into a 3-4-3 - called the W-M because the shape it formed spelled out the letters - is generally believed to belong to a man called Herbert Chapman, who was once controversially banned from soccer for life.

4. WEST SIDE STORY

"I felt, I knew something never before was going to happen, had to happen. But this is so much more."

~ TONY, *West Side Story*

"It's one-nil to the Arsenal. That's the way we like it"

~ GEORGE ALLISON

Herbert Chapman has one of those big blue plaques you see in London and other places around the United Kingdom. They are permanent historical markers installed to commemorate the link between the place and a famous person, like the brass stars on Hollywood Boulevard. Chapman joins Sir Winston Churchill, Charlie Chaplin and Keith Moon in having his own plaque, so it is quite a big deal. While history also credits Chapman with the invention of the tactics board, white balls instead of dark ones and floodlit matches, it is his contribution to tactics for which he is immortalized. He was the first to question whether adequate credit was given to defending.

Like Meisl and Hogan, Chapman's journeyman playing career was not what earned him his plaque. In fact, when he originally hung up his boots, it was not for retirement, or even management, but for engineering. That idea lasted just a few weeks, as his head was soon turned by the chance to stagger his retirement with a player-manager role at his old club Northampton Town. The insight that kindled his managerial career was that it was possible for a team to spend too much time and effort relentlessly attacking and not enough on the more intellectual pursuit of organizing a victory.

After leading Northampton to a Southern League title, Chapman moved on to Leeds City, where he took them from the foot of Division Two (what is currently known as the English Championship) to fourth place. But then he was implicated in a scandal involving illegal payments to players. Leeds City were kicked out of the league and Chapman banned in disgrace because he refused to hand over the club's record books. That might have been that, had Huddersfield Town not come knocking two years later. After a successful appeal to the FA, Chapman was back in the game. He promptly won the FA Cup, followed by two First Division titles in four years. With a feather in his cap, Chapman headed south, to Arsenal, in the summer of 1925.

"I am going to make this the greatest club in the world," Chapman had said when he took the job at Highbury. In his first season, Chapman steered Arsenal to an FA Cup quarter final and a second-place finish in the First Division (now the Premier League); the highest league placing in their history. Historians point knowingly to the influence of his first signing, the tall and technically excellent Charlie Buchan. The 1.9m, 172 lbs frontman aligned tactically with Chapman, pointing out that although the new offside law meant withdrawing a centre-half from midfield was essential, it left teams at a numerical disadvantage in midfield.

The former Sunderland man was 34 when he joined Arsenal, an advanced age for a player even now, and his proposed solution was that he take on the responsibility of dropping back from his inside right position to form a 3-3-4. Chapman conjured a compromise, suggesting a 3-2-2-3 shape instead, leaving Buchan high up the field and instead asking third team player Andy Neil to play the withdrawn role. Buchan went on to score 56 goals in 120 games for Arsenal before retiring in 1928 aged 36.

When Chapman agreed to join Arsenal, he had asked for the time necessary to build an efficient machine. Like pistons gathering speed, what happened after he joined was slow, and then spectacular. Buchan's replacement was Scotsman Alex James, signed for £9,000 from Preston. The club's official history sees James as the key man in Arsenal's subsequent success. Chapman's genius was not in shifting the emphasis from attack to defence, but from attack to counter-attack. He wanted numerical superiority not in midfield, but where it mattered most: the penalty areas. His side drew opponents towards their own goal, stifling the attack before breaking quickly and mercilessly with long passes to the wings.

Brian Glanville, who attended Charterhouse school, where the game was played in the 19th Century, wrote in his book *The Real Arsenal:* "Though his Arsenal teams would in due course score a multitude of goals, he'd tell his teams that when they went out on the field, they went out with one point. If they didn't give away a goal, they'd come off with at least one point. Even if his team won, he would insist on a tight defence. Eddie Hapgood recalled an occasion when, after the team had one handsomely, Chapman subsequently harangued them in his office for an hour, declaring that the one goal they gave away should not have been conceded."

On joining Arsenal in 1996, a fan asked Arsene Wenger about Chapman. "Ah yes, he's the man who put numbers on players' shirts and changed the metro station name from Gillespie Road to Arsenal." Wenger himself understood how to have an impact, calibrating the players' diets and putting an end to the Highbury booze culture by shutting down the players' bar. For both men, success could be found through discipline and innovation. Wenger's Arsenal side that went through the 2003-2004 season unbeaten - The Invincibles - has a strong claim to be the best side ever seen in the Premier League. Their style had a clear tactical identity, with a focus on pace, the use of inside runs from wide, overlapping full-backs and the drifting positions of the forwards. At the core of it all was a Chapman hallmark: aggressive counter attacking.

Britain's economy in the 1920s was struggling to bankroll the aftermath of World War I. The Wall Street Crash of 1929 caused a slump in world trade. Prices fell and credit dried up, but there was no Great Depression in North London. Arsenal won the FA Cup in 1930, the league in 1931, 1933, 1934, 1935, and 1938, while also lifting the FA Cup again in 1936. It is true that Chapman had first used the W-M with his Huddersfield Town side, but there are some legitimate historical question marks over whether or not Chapman actually 'invented' it. In 2011, journalist Jonathan Wilson, author of the peerless *Inverting The Pyramid*, discovered a column written in the *Southampton Football Echo* in 1925 which contained strong evidence that he did not. A person going by the name of "Cherry Blossom" wrote that Southampton's loss to Bradford City as far back as September 25, 1925 was down to tactics:

"There is a lot of talk in the dressing rooms at the moment over what is known as the W formation in attack to deal with the changed conditions of play. In this formation the centre-forward and the two extreme wingers go well up the field – staying only a yard or so onside – and the two inside wing-forwards remain behind, acting as five-eighths, or in others words operating in a sphere of play near the half-backs and behind the three advanced forwards."

So even though the W-M concept was alive and kicking as early as 1925, we also know that newspapers largely ignored this shift. They printed line-ups in a stock 2-3-5 formation until the 1960s. Perhaps it was due to conservatism, or a general stubbornness to even acknowledge the development of tactics. Maybe they simply could not be bothered to change the print layout. Whatever the reason, English soccer was not ready to nurture a progressive mind. The FA, having publicly admonished his Huddersfield Town side's 1922 FA Cup final win for what they perceived as niggly fouls, also resisted Chapman's moves to introduce shirt numbers and floodlit matches. They say that history is written by the victors, so it is reasonable to conclude that because Arsenal were the first team to prosper under the W-M branding, it is to Chapman - who became known as the 'Napoleon of North London' - that the victory parade points.

"It works. I am just waiting until everyone has copied it, then I shall come up with something new," said Chapman. Sadly, he never had the chance to move onto the next big thing, dying prematurely of pneumonia on 6 January, 1934, just a couple of weeks short of his fifty-sixth birthday. A tireless worker, he became ill after watching a game of juniors in the wet. But arguably his work was already done. In shifting soccer's emphasis from individuality and artistic expressions to systems and tactics, he did not need to. He had dragged the conversation up to a better vantage point, from which history could see to the rest.

5. THE BIG HEAT

"Ale makes men foolish, but coffee makes them dangerous."
~ PETER, *The Bitter Trade*

"You don't always get what you wish for. Especially in Nazi Germany."
~ MARKUS ZUSAK

Chapman's rise and premature death left a huge question mark over the trajectory of tactical thinking about the game. Soccer was born in the public schools, but by the time Arsenal were in full swing, it was very much a working-class sport and the de facto topic of conversation in the pub. To make the leap forward, it required adoption by a demographic that could chaperone this intellectual shift. This book's own pathfinder, Jonathan Wilson, pinpoints this metamorphosis to the coffee houses of 1930s Vienna.

Americans might drink more coffee than any other nation today - and the average New Yorker seven times more than any other U.S.

city - but US adoption was a century behind the Viennese. The transition from tea to coffee traces back to 1773, when political protesters threw stealthily-taxed British tea into Massachusetts Bay. After that, it became something of a patriotic duty to drink coffee instead. Soccer is now trendy among artists, writers and actors, and its ascent is arguably thanks not to Starbucks or even hipsters, but the soldiers of the Ottoman Turkish army.

When the soldiers abandoned their siege of the Austrian capital in 1683, they left behind large sacks of coffee beans. A couple of years later the first coffee house opened, and within 200 years they had spread like wildfire throughout the city. Unlike Britain, where drinking and then sometimes singing and vomiting was done in the pub, in central Europe coffee-houses flourished as a hub for both men and women of all classes to congregate, debate and get a cup of joe. Art, poetry, philosophy and politics were discussed, so it was natural that soccer, which is made of the same threads, weaved its way into the fabric of society.

In 1898, workers in a Viennese factory formed a club called Wiener Arbeiter FK, which you might know today as Rapid Vienna, while Austria Vienna was a club with strong support from the Jewish bourgeoisie. In 1909, the Star of David was sewn into players' shirts to form a Jewish club called Hakoah Wien. Many of the clubs had their own coffee houses in the city, but one seemed to unite them all: the Ring Café, which became the unofficial headquarters of the game in Austria.

It was in the Ring Café that an event took place which today could perhaps only happen through social media. It involved a growing consensus that despite the upward trajectory of Meisl's *Wunderteam* in the 1920s, the missing piece of the puzzle was the stick-thin but extraordinary forward, Matthias Sindelar of Austria Vienna. Sindelar, the theatre critic Alfred Polgar noted, "had brains in his legs and many remarkable and unexpected things occurred to them while they were running."

For all his physical frailty, his peerless speed and ingenuity meant that the Ring Café wanted him at the apex of the Austrian side. The coffee-houses saw him as soccer's embodiment of Mozart or a chess grandmaster. 'Der Papierene' - 'the Paper-man' simply had to play. The only problem was that Meisl thought otherwise. He wasn't opposed to Sindelar's gifts - he had given him his Austrian debut in 1926 - but despite operating at the highest level of the game, he was essentially a conservative coach. For years he resisted the clamor of the coffee-houses to recall Sindelar, until one afternoon he was physically surrounded in the Ring Cafe. David Goldblatt described the events in *The Ball is Round: A Global History of Soccer:*

"Meisl was cornered by a gathering of the city's leading soccer commentators as he sat in the Ring Café in 1931. Everyone was arguing for Sindelar's recall and Meisl changed his mind. Sindelar played. Scotland were beaten and the *Wunderteam* - already disciplined, organized, hardworking and professional - acquired their playmaker and inspiration, that vital spark of unpredictability."

Scotland weren't just beaten, they were thumped 5-0 and in the same week that England also lost to France in Paris. It was the middle of May 1931 and a watershed moment for the European press, who were eager to point out to Britain that it was no longer possible to deny that the world had caught up. Austria went the next eleven games unbeaten with Sindelar at the heart of a team and then faced England at Chelsea's Stamford Bridge in December 1932. They lost 4-3, but this time the British press took note. Austria had impressed and

Manchester United offered Sindelar the chance to play in England. He declined.

Meisl yearned for victory over the English, and he achieved it inside Vienna's Praterstadion in the hot Spring of 1936. It was a 2-1 win in which Austria were now significantly superior, with the Danubian school of soccer set to become the outstanding reference for teams across Europe in the years that followed.

The inevitable decline of the *Wunderteam* coincided with the rise of fascism in Europe, where the politics of Mussolini in Italy and Franco in Spain were characterised by cynical, physically aggressive and successful national sides. Italy won the first two World Cups, in 1934 and 1938, before World War II interrupted international competition. The closing scene of soccer's first act belongs to Sindelar the Paper Man, who ended his career by lighting a torch to fascism, and in doing so thrust soccer into the the geo-political limelight for the first time.

The coffee houses had been thrilled when Sindelar's success gave them a personal stake in the fortunes of the national team. Similarly, Sindelar felt for this community when the Nazi tanks stood poised to roll in and ruin everything. When Austria was annexed into the German Reich on March 12, 1938, the newly formed National Socialist Government quickly disbanded the country's professional league and expelled the Jewish clubs. They saw in the *Wunderteam* a propaganda opportunity; a fully-formed marquee acquisition that would be simple to rebrand as their own.

Sindelar, the son of a blacksmith, was born in Moravia, in the eastern part of the old Czech Republic and all records suggest that the family was not Jewish, but Catholic. His father was killed on the Italian front during World War I, so perhaps it was a combined distaste for war and natural Social Democratic leanings that resulted in his refusal to play for a new 'united' German team. In any case, any player or indeed official of Jewish ethnicity was ostracized.. Some wisely fled, others remained.

With Austria becoming a province of the German Reich, Sindelar had initially refused to join the German national team. But he did agree to take part in a showcase reunification derby - Austria against Germany, on the condition that Austria be allowed to play in their traditional colors. The authorities had decreed that a low-scoring draw would be a suitable reunification scoreline. But that's not what happened.

The Ostmark XI were a significantly better side than the Germans, so it was hard to disguise the talent gap. From newspaper reports, we know that Sindelar missed a hatful of chances in the first half. Perhaps the reality has been embellished by myth, but you can find some sources that suggest Sindelar's misses were deliberate mockery. Stephen Tudor, writing in *These Football Times,* suggested: "With gleeful devilment Sindelar spurned a host of simple chances throughout the first half, placing the ball inches wide on each occasion as if to illustrate just how easy it all was for the grandmaster against the supposed master race."

Sindelar's misses are a grey area, but what we do know is that he did eventually find the target, tucking a rebound away in the second half. His strike partner Schati Sesta added a second from distance, and, to the horror of Nazi dignitaries in the director's box, Sindelar celebrated by dancing a taunting little jig in front of them. Less than a year later, he was dead.

Sindelar owned a cafe, and the authorities had noted him as a troublemaker when he was reluctant to put up Nazi posters on the walls. In the wake of his jig in Vienna, Sindelar had continued to refuse to play for the united German team, insisting that he was now retired and, with his hair now slicked down to denote respectability - but perhaps not humility - happy to bus tables rather than kick soccer balls and serve coffee to customers who had only recently paid just to see his wispy form in the flesh.

On January 23 1939, Sindelar was found naked and dead in the arms of his Jewish girlfriend Camilla Castignola, the victim of carbon monoxide poisoning. She died a week later. Like Sindelar's first-half misses, it is not known whether his death was deliberate or accidental. It may have been murder, it may have been suicide, or it may have been nothing more than a faulty heater, but soccer had died in Vienna.

6. THE EMPIRE STRIKES BACK

"First, you must unlearn what you've learned."
~ YODA, *The Empire Strikes Back*

"Some people are on the pitch! They think it's all over. It is now."
~ KENNETH WOLSTENHOLME, BBC Commentator

With the Second World War in the rearview mirror, in 1950 the England squad arrived at their maiden World Cup in Brazil after missing the first three tournaments. The self-proclaimed 'Kings of Soccer' simply didn't enter the first three, but had come to prove that they were the world's best and to take home the Jules Rimet trophy. Italy had won the tournament twelve years previously in France, beating Hungary 4-2 in the final. When they handed officials the trophy to mark the beginning of the World Cup, many assumed it would be only a matter of time before it was in the hands of England captain, Billy Wright. But the USA had other ideas.

The Americans had given the Spanish a bumpy opening game, going down 3-1, but England posed a sterner test. "We were still feeling pretty good about ourselves, because we had really scared the hell out of Spain," said defender Harry Keough before the game in Belo Horizonte. "We certainly didn't entertain any ideas that we were going to beat them, but we figured we could give them a battle for it." The US were a team of amateurs. The England team were a team of superstars, including names like Stanley Matthews and Tom Finney who were famous around the world. But the 'Wizard of the Dribble' Matthews wasn't named in the team that day after being forced by the FA to go on a goodwill tour of Canada. Matthews won two league titles 30 years apart with Stoke City and continued playing professionally until he was 50, taking care of his body in a way that preceded sports science. He was exceptional, but this was 20 years before the introduction of substitutes to the game, so no Matthews in the starting line-up meant he wasn't going to feature at all.

"According to everybody who ever wrote about Stanley Matthews, he was probably one of the greatest talents there ever was," said Keogh. "Had he played, the chances are they would have won. But the chances are they would have won anyway." Keogh had a point. The US were 500-1 outsiders for the tournament, while England were at 3-1 and had won 23 out of 30 matches since the war, including wins home and away against the mighty Italians.

England controlled the early exchanges, with six shots on goal in the opening twelve minutes. But the USA held firm, and as half-time approached, there was a rare American attack, with captain Walter Bahr trying his luck from outside the area. "Joe Gaetjens dives at it. He doesn't head the ball, but the ball just snips his head," said Keogh. "The ball changed direction and speed. The goalie Bert Williams was on the ground and nobody knew where the hell it went until they saw it bouncing up and down in the net. That was in the 37th minute. The English got a little mad about that."

Humiliating as the 1950 defeat was, apart from a defeat to the Republic of Ireland at Everton's Goodison Park in 1949, England had never lost at home to foreign opposition before. Sindelar's *Wunderteam* had beaten England in Vienna, but no team had done it at Wembley, or the Empire Stadium as it was known then. In 1952, the writer Ivan Sharpe, who won Olympic Gold as a player with Great Britain at the 1912 Olympics in Sweden, expressed concerns about the stagnation of English soccer. "Other countries are now way ahead of us in terms of the soccer they play,' he wrote. A year later, Hungary's 'Golden Squad' came to town. They were the Olympic champions up against the game's progenitors in their own back yard. The press billed it as 'the Match of the Century'. While from a distance it's easy to recognise this as the hype machine doing its thing, looking back no result has so reverberated through soccer history.

On the same pitch six months earlier, four of the England team had played in the FA Cup final as Matthews' Stoke came from 3-1 down to beat Blackpool 4-3. It was the same year as the coronation of Queen Elizabeth I and that Sir Edmund Hillary became the first man to conquer Mt. Everest, so it seemed natural that England would assert her dominance in the showpiece game. Instead, they were beaten. And not just beaten but flummoxed, baffled and humiliated in a defeat that Glanville wrote "gave eyes to the blind".

It was a defeat that was both technical and tactical. Lionel Messi and Cristiano Ronaldo's goalscoring records are impressive feats, but at the time of writing they're not yet within touching distance of the great Ferenc Puskas, who scored 746 goals in 709 games for Real

Madrid and Hungary. The English might have been professionally warmed by the sight of Puskas offhandedly performing keepie-uppies while he waited to kick off, but they were knocked clean cold by what followed. Hungary had some of the greatest players in the world at the time and their technical superiority was married with Gusztáv Sebes, an inspirational and meticulous coach.

The England team, playing a W-M, lacked cohesion. If the defeat can generally be chalked up as a victory of teamwork and fluidity over the hard-hitting British method, it can be specifically pinpointed to Sebes' decision to play forward Nandor Hidegkuti sitting deep as a 'false nine' in a 2-3-3-2 formation. England, playing a centre back Harry Johnston, were lost. If he followed him down the pitch the two full backs were left with a gaping hole in the middle, and if he stayed where he was, Hidegkuti was left with the full expanse of Wembley to roam. Johnston later said "the tragedy was the utter helplessness" and England lost 6-3. If you were a fan looking regrettably over your shoulder at the stadium's forlorn two towers on the way home, and if you had the right kind of eyes, you could see the high water mark, that place where the wave of British dominion over soccer finally broke, and rolled back. It was 25 November, 1953.

This humbling, interpreted by some as a victory for socialism against an imperial Britain with her tail between her legs, led to a bit of a rethink. England, unsurprisingly, lost the rematch 7-1 in Budapest the following year. Some habitual thinkers wanted a return to the 2-3-5 of the golden age of when England used to win, others who were more progressive but lacking in imagination simply wanted to copy the Hungarians.

There was one man, however, who saw things differently. He didn't subscribe to the accepted truth that Hungary had outthought and outclassed England. Instead, he dug his heels in and attributed the defeat to the notion that Hungary had just had one of those days when everything they hit ended up in the back of the net. The statistics refute this, because in light of the fact that Hungary had 35 shots to England's five, 6-3 was a blessing. In normal circumstances this man would be laughed out of this book, but his name is Sir Alf Ramsey, and he was playing right back.

After a successful managerial spell at Ipswich that *The Times* wrote defied explanation, Ramsey succeeded the Dickensially named Walter Winterbottom as England manager. It was 1962, and if things went according to plan, Ramsey would be in charge for the World Cup on home soil. He experimented with both a W-M (under duress from an FA committee) and a 4-2-4, before switching to a 4-3-3, a system which shunned wingers at a time when the rest of the world was still in love with them.

Ramsey's 'Wingless Wonders', as they were later dubbed, beat Spain 2-0 in December 1965. It was a performance of such fearsome promise that Ramsey immediately bottled it up and reverted to 4-2-4 for the next game, telling British newspaper *The Mail*, "I think it would be quite wrong to let the rest of the world, our rivals, see what we are doing. My job will be to produce the right team at the right time and that does not always mean pressing ahead with a particular combination just because it has been successful."

Ramsey kept his cards close to his chest, tinkering with the formation and personnel right up until the final warm up game against Poland in Katowice, a 1-0 victory. In the group stage, England drew 0-0 with Uruguay and beat Mexico and France 2-0 before overcoming Argentina in a bloodthirsty quarter final which, amidst the backdrop of the Falklands War, Hugh McIlvanney described as "not so much a soccer match as an international incident." In the semi-final, Captain Bobby Moore stifled Portugal's 'Black Pearl' Eusebio, guiding England to a 2-1 win. Finally, West Germany were defeated 4-2, a result which brought color back to the cheeks of a nation that had been so humbled in Belo Horizonte 16 years before.

7. THE QUICK AND THE DEAD

"I'm so damned fast I can wake up at the crack of dawn, rob two banks, a train and a stage coach, shoot the tail feathers off a duck's ass at 300 feet, and still be back in bed before you wake up next to me."

~ KID, *The Quick and the Dead*

"The best moment to win the ball is immediately after your team just lost it. The opponent is still looking for orientation where to pass the ball. He will have taken his eyes off the game to make his tackle or interception and he will have expended energy. Both make him vulnerable."

~ JURGEN KLOPP

Normally, it's hard to divine when you're living through a revolutionary period; it's far easier to connect the dots going backwards. When England won the World Cup, the average distance covered in a match was 5.5 km. To watch a rerun of that game is to witness a surprisingly pedestrian encounter compared to the velocity of today's Premier League. Some 25 years later, that distance had jumped to around 9km. At the time of writing, players

are covering about 11.5 km in 90 minutes. The shift can be characterised by two changes.

First, developments in sports science mean players are simply fitter
than they used to be. They can run faster and further and recover
quicker. The second is tactics. Once someone had the idea to allow
the opposition less time on the ball, to reduce the space in which they
could move during that time and to hurry them into making deci-
sions, that set in motion a sequence of events that you'd be hard
pressed to deny makes the game everything it is today. You've learnt
about Jimmy Hogan, Hugo Meisl, Herbert Chapman and Sir Alf
Ramsey. The next name on the altar of soccer's tactics board is the
amiable Russian, Viktor Maslov.

Maslov was born in Moscow in the spring of 1910, just six months
before Theodore Roosevelt became the first former president to ride
in an airplane, accepting an invitation from the Wright Brothers'
young aviator trainee Arch Hoxsey in Missouri. "Soccer is like an
airplane," said Maslov, incidentally. "As velocities increase, so does air
resistance, and so you need to make the head more streamlined." In a
childhood surrounded by the spectre of war and revolutionary
energy a mind was forged that brought tactical innovation to the
game as we know it today. To cut, as it were, to the chase... he
invented pressing.

After his playing career with Torpedo Moscow ended in 1942, Maslov
took over as coach, inspiring great loyalty from his players and
managing Torpedo in four separate spells before taking the helm at
Dynamo Kyiv in 1964. His appointment coincided with a growing
understanding of the components of physical performance. To press,
players have to very fit. So for it to enter soccer's tactical sphere
required the coaches managing their fitness to have an advanced

knowledge of physical conditioning and nutrition. This was now available. It didn't resemble today's knowledge, but in 150 years things will look quite different too. The point is that when leveraged, it had powerful consequences.

Maslov's teams began to harass and hustle the opposition high up the pitch, using improved physical fitness and organizational qualities to fill the space on the pitch vacated by the jostlers. The result was that there was less time and space for players to take actions. For both teams, with and without the ball, this meant that positioning, timing, direction, speed, decision making and execution all had to improve. As a result of teams being being able to pass, press and tackle better, the game was played at a higher tempo, which is to say a higher *quantity* of *quality* actions. For example, professional players might be able to make four actions per minute with an average of 15 seconds between actions, while amateur players can only make two actions per minute, and require 30 seconds of rest between actions.

This is the seismic shift Maslov brought to the game, and yet the Moscovite press was horrified. One newspaper printed a picture of four of Maslov's players hounding an opponent captioned: "We don't need this kind of soccer." There are people who will pin their flag to a mast and tell you that is was not Maslov's Dynamo but Arrigo Sacchi's AC Milan (which we'll learn about in *Modern Times*) in the late 80s that deserve the credit. It's possible to counter these claims. Maslov had studied the Brazilian 4-2-4 at the 1958 World Cup and seen the importance of bringing one of the forwards back to play in a three-man midfield when the game demanded it. If all Maslov did was improve his team's fitness, then that's less a soccer achievement than a physiological one. But he also invented a tactical system that made room for a playmaker's creative qualities to roam. Pressing might have been a fitness-oriented innovation, but its motivation was tactical. So too was pushing his wingers inside to operate more as wide midfielders, allowing room for a second striker to play in between the lines. When Maslov did that, he invented the 4-4-2.

The 4-4-2 has become something of a default soccer formation. It's simple, easy to understand and execute, particularly at youth level, either as a 'flat four' midfield or a 'diamond', pairing a defensive-minded destroyer with a more attacking-minded player in behind the strikers. It suits players who can play in wide positions and make the pitch big, as well as good crossers of the ball, taking advantage of gaps generated in the opposition's defensive line. And on a very simple level, it's arguably easier to score goals and win games with two strikers than with one.

And win Maslov did. His Dynamo side dominated Soviet soccer with three consecutive league titles between 1966 and 1968 through team performances that demonstrated exceptional organization. He also revived a couple of aborted USSR experiments with defensive zonal marking. Man marking, Maslov famously said, "humiliates, insults and even morally oppresses the players who resort to it." He built a side that was able to nullify opposition movement with the quality of their positioning and exhaust them with the intensity of their press-ing. In the 1966-67 season, Dynamo conceded just eleven goals.

In the seven years he was in charge in Kiev, Maslov inspired great affection from his players, some of whom called him Grandad. But after the World Cup in Mexico in 1970, Maslov found himself without key players for six weeks and results started to slide. "After the second half of the season we were second in the table, and I'm sure Grandad would have kept his job if we'd maintained that position to the end," said defender Viktor Matviyenko. "But Grandad brought straight back players who had lost their sharpness, and so we began to fall in the standings. "

Despite having challenged and eventually dethroned the Moscow elite in his seven years at the club, Dynamo were ruthless when results started to slip. They announced that Maslov had been removed from his position before an away game against CSKA Moscow. There was no replacement named and Maslov watched his team lose 1-0 as a spectator in the stand. The club dropped him off at the metro station on the way home, while the players and other staff flew back to Kyiv. It was a particularly cruel goodbye.

Unfortunately, there was no comeback story. Maslov returned to Moscow in 1972 for another spell with Torpedo, but failed to turn them into a title-winning team. He may have run out of ideas, or his heart was broken by the betrayal, but Grandad could not muster the energy for a new project. His last job, with FC Ararat Yerevan in what is modern day Armenia, was his last. He retired in 1975, and passed away two years later.

Ironically, Maslov's legacy is personified in a player he ultimately fell out with, Valeriy Lobanovskyi. The apocryphal story goes that Lobanovsky, a hugely talented and effective left winger, declined to toast to his teammates' good luck with some Ukrainian horilka (a spirit similar to vodka) after a team flight had been delayed. Lobanovskyi was known to be fastidious, but after the incident, the two never saw eye to eye again. The player left the club not long after he was substituted for the first time in his career, having given Dynamo the lead against Spartak Moscow in April 1964.

But he remained a disciple. Brazil may have celebrated the 'banana' shot more than any other team, but it was Lobanovskyi, once a student of heating engineering at the Kyivan Polytechnic Institute, who invented it. After he retired aged 29, he went on to become the most successful manager in Soviet and Ukrainian history. He joined FC Dnipro Dnipropetrovsk for four quiet years, before taking over at Dynamo Kyiv. In 1975, his side became the first from the Soviet Union to win a major European trophy, beating Hungarian side Ferenváros 3-0 in the Cup Winner's Cup final in Basel. To this, he added five league titles.

As a player Lobanovskyi had been an individual and a trickster, but as a coach he was a revolutionary, combining the scientific methods he had studied in Kyiv with extreme disciplinary rigour. The results were emphatic. During two spells in Kyiv (he managed the USSR between 1983 and 1984), he not so much broke the Russian dominance of Soviet soccer but pummeled into submission. He led his side to the Soviet super league eight times, the cup six times, the European Cup Winners' Cup of 1975 and 1986, and European Super Cup of 1975. "A path always remains a path," he said. "It's a path during the day, it's a path during the night and it's a path during the dawn.

8. THE ITALIAN JOB

"I trust everyone. It's the devil inside them I don't trust."
   ~ JOHN BRIDGER, *The Italian Job*

"We have never heard the devil's side of the story, God wrote all the book."
   ~ ANATOLE FRANCE

When Manchester United beat Liverpool 2-1 at Old Trafford in early March 2018, fans and pundits lamented a frustrating game to watch. Liverpool has 68 percent possession and 14 shots to United's five, but United goalkeeper David De Gea was not required to make a single save. When Liverpool did find the net, it was through an own goal by United defender Eric Bailly. "Against Liverpool if you play bad when you have the ball you can be in trouble," Mourinho told the Sky Sports cameras. "In the second half it was not our intention - I cannot say this was the plan. Liverpool pushed us into defensive situation but we kept control. It was a complete performance by us with two different halves. If people don't think we deserved it, I don't care."

Fans of modern soccer who recognise - and feel frustration with - the fundamental clash of ideologies between Mourinho and Liverpool manager Jurgen Klopp, Mourinho and Pep Guardiola, Mourinho and just about everyone who goes out to try and win a game rather than waiting for the opposition to die of boredom, might like to be able to tell people where exactly this clash of ideologies started.

To do so, we need to look to a man called Helenio Herrera, who managed Inter Milan in the 1960s. Born in Buenos Aires to Spanish migrant parents, his father was an exiled anarchist carpenter from Andalusia and his mother a cleaner with 'extraordinary intelligence'. The family moved to Morocco when Herrera was young, where his soccer education matched the ethnic diversity of his neighbourhood. He told journalist Simon Kuper, "From fourteen or fifteen years old, I played with the Arabs, Jews, with the French and Spaniards. That is the school of life." He was tough and aggressive, but a playing career that started in Casablanca and took him to France never amounted to much and was cut short, like so many, by a serious knee injury.

He had managerial spells in France, before moving to Spain and managing Real Valladaolid, Atlético Madrid, Malaga, Deportivo la Coruña, Sevilla and Barcelona, picking up four La Liga titles along the way. Success in Catalonia prompted a lucrative offer from Inter, a then-record annual salary of $43,000. He would spend the next eight years in the north of Italy, winning three *Serie A* titles and two European Cups. In doing so, he became a superstar, transcending the notion that managers were marginal figures in a team. But he is also remembered as the high priest of cynical, negative, ruthless soccer. How did this happen? And is this legacy justified?

The first thing to know is that Herrera is synonymous with a system called *catenaccio*, an Italian world which means 'door-bolt'. In turn, *catenaccio* comes from the French word *verrou* (also door-bolt in translation), a defensive setup invented by Austrian coach Karl Rappan. He was member of the Danubian school we visited in *The Graduate*, a tactical mind that developed in Viennese coffee house society. The difference was that his interpretation of the game was more defensive than romantic. He may not have known it at the time, but his tactics spawned what some came to interpret as evil.

As coach of Switzerland in the 1930s and 1940s, Rappan played a defensive sweeper called the *verouilleur*, planted between the goalkeeper and three defenders. It was a defensive modification of the 3-2-5 W-M, inserting an extra player behind the last line to form a 1-3-2-4. Ironically the system originated from Rappan's time as player coach of Swiss side Servette, and the need to make his semi-professional players match up against the fitness of professional sides. Later, as coach of Switzerland, he led his country to the 1938 World Cup and an honourable quarter-final exit to Hungary. Taking *verrou* to the world stage was an achievement much grander than its original purpose.

When Hererra joined Inter, he did so knowing that the president, Angelo Moratti, had sacked twelve coaches in five years. Nearly fifty years later, it would be Moratti's son, Massimo, who sat in the president's chair and watched with glee as Mourinho guided Inter to two *Serie A* titles, the Supercoppa Italiana, the Coppa Italia and the UEFA Champions League in two spectacular years. The parallels with Mourinho are hard to ignore. Both have been called tyrannical and ruthless. Both have a well-documented obsession with detail, preparation and opposition dossiers. Both loved discipline, psychology and, crucially, winning trophies.

Herrera's *Internazionale* threw a shadow over their illustrious neighbour A.C. Milan by winning three Scudettos and back-to-back European Cups, but only after Herrera himself narrowly avoided the sack. He played attacking soccer in the first two seasons, but despite scoring lots of goals, it only yielded second and third-place finishes. Moratti felt change was necessary, and went as far as to invite former Inter player Edmondo Fabbri to Milan to offer him Herrera's job before changing his mind. Herrera changed his, too, becoming the master of 1-0 wins, even against the strongest attacks. His *catenaccio* was an exercise in extreme thoroughness. Whereas Rapan had three defenders, Hererra set up *four* to man mark opposition attackers, then employed an extra player - a sweeper, Armando Picchi - to pick up any loose balls that managed to penetrate. So *catenaccio* was *verrou* + 1.

Playing a back five liberated the left back to attack more or less at will, with the freedom of space and the benefit of a picture of the pitch in front of him. The left back blessed with this opportunity was Giacino Facchetti, who had originally signed for Inter as a forward. He responded to this role by hitting double figures as a left-back, something unheard of in *Serie A*. In his book, *The Legendary Ten: From Humble Beginnings to Big Business*, Brian Boedker quotes Herrera: "In attack, all the players knew what I wanted: vertical soccer at great speed, with no more than three passes to get to the opponent's box. If you lose the ball playing vertically, it's not a problem - but lose it laterally and you pay with a goal." Or, more succinctly: "He'd train our brains before our legs," said forward Sandro Mazzola.

For Herrera, "Class + Preparation + Intelligence + Athleticism = Championships." He stuck this slogan on the walls of the ground and made the players chant it during training sessions. On the one hand, he was revolutionary. He insisted that his players concentrate for three straight days before a game, confining them to the Appiano Gentile training headquarters where he could control their sleep, diet and psychological inputs. On the other, with his rigour came suggestions that Herrera was doping his players.

In 2015, Mazzola's brother Ferruccio gave an interview to the Italian magazine *Espresso* in which he claimed that Herrera was putting something in the pre-training coffee: "I do not know for sure what was inside," said Mazzola, who was playing in the Inter reserves at the time. "I think they were amphetamines. He experimented with them on the reserves. Once, after drinking the coffee before we played Como in 1967, I was in a state of total hallucination for three days and nights, like an epileptic. Since this story came out, Sandro and I do not talk anymore. He says I have washed the family's dirty clothes in public."

Amphetamine and its derivatives, like phentermine and ephedrine, are stimulants that impact the central nervous system, generally increasing alertness and decreasing appetite. In the US, their use was normalized for soldiers during World War II, then fueled by marketing and loosely prescribed by doctors to combat middle class weight worries. According to the National Center for Biotechnology Information, by 1970, five percent of Americans - nearly 10 million - used prescription amphetamines, and 3.2 million were addicted.

In a wider context, it doesn't take a big jump in imagination to believe the rumours about Il Caffè Herrera, because any tactical superiority multiplied by physical advantage was likely to yield results. On the other hand, if you reverse that logic, you could end up accusing any team with tactical success of taking stimulants. According to FIFA's recent doping numbers, amphetamine use in global soccer is not as widespread as public consumption in the US. While the US saw a 53% rise in prescription amphetamines to treat ADHD between 2018 and 2012, FIFA carried out over 31,242 global doping tests in 2014, with just 61 samples (0.2%) testing positive. But let's not forget that that Diego Maradona was kicked out of the US World Cup in 1994 for testing positive for ephedrine. If the greatest in the world can be tempted by a marginal advantage, anyone can.

Doping allegations aside, history has not been kind to a man who won as many titles as Herrera did. Arguably Mourinho is headed in the same direction, so it's appropriate that Herrerra's spirit is echoed in Mourinho's rhetoric today. "Modestly, I've won more than any other manager in the world. My case is unprecedented." Herrera said this, but it could so believably have been Mourinho that it's hard not to raise a wry smile at the similarities in their defensive lines.

9. COMING TO AMERICA

"The royal penis is clean, your Highness."
~ BATHER, *Coming to America*

"People argue between Pelé or Maradona. Di Stéfano is the best, much more complete."
~ PELÉ

Researching the development of soccer's administrative roots in the US is a tortuous undertaking. It's characterised by regional disputes, competing bodies, the onset of the Great Depression and the extraordinarily long arm of FIFA. It took awhile for soccer to plant seed in America, but when it did, it was spectacular.

Long before soccer, there was Pasuckuakohowog, a Native American term which literally translates as "they gather the ball with the foot." There's evidence that it was played as early as the 17th Century, when it was played on beaches with goals nearly a kilometer wide and set twice as far apart. Some games had up to 1000 players and the spectacle was more like war than sport. But kicking something with your foot was where the similarities ended.

A soccer that you would identify with more arrived in the United States in the mid-19th Century. The beautiful game came to the Land of the Free in the same way it had traveled throughout the rest of the world: as a British export. It landed in the deep-water port of New Orleans. There are records of a first US match 'inspired' by the FA rules taking place between the universities of Princeton and Rutgers in November 1869, but this wasn't quite soccer either, because each side had 25 players. Other colleges followed suit, but had converted to rugby within a few years and these teams would soon form the bedrock of American football.

In 1921, the country's first proper soccer competition, the American Soccer League (ASL) was formed with founding teams hailing from industrial towns such as Fall River, Massachusetts and Bethlehem, Pennsylvania. Some clubs were even able to attract European talent with the bolt-on promise of a guaranteed well-paying factory job. The US finished third at the inaugural 1930 World Cup in Uruguay, which didn't feature many of the top European teams, but even so, this was no meagre beginning.

By 1931, infighting between the leagues, the clubs and the national federation caused the ASL to collapse like a soufflé. Obscurity beckoned. If the US hadn't chalked their miracle victory over England we learnt about in *The Empire Strikes Back*, who knows when or even if soccer would have set foot in the American psyche ever again. It wasn't until late 1960s that there was another crack at a professional league. A group of entrepreneurs launched the National Professional Soccer League (NPSL) in 1967 after securing a contract from broadcast network CBS, albeit without FIFA's permission. It was called the

National Professional Soccer League (NPSL) and it lasted just one season. The head of CBS at the time, Bill McPhail, later told *Sports Illustrated*, "The stadiums were empty, which made it tough for us to generate much excitement. The players had foreign names, their faces were unfamiliar, their backgrounds undistinguished." It wouldn't stay that way.

Between 1976 and 1981, it rained soccer royalty on the United States. Pelé, George Best and Johan Cruyff, three of the greatest players the world has ever seen, let alone three of the greatest players of the time, contributed to a legacy that would ignite America's soccer boom. For an amazing number of reasons, apart from those that are comically obvious given McPhail's experience, the significance of this trilogy of fortune can hardly be overstated. Imagine, for a moment, that all of a sudden, Lionel Messi, Cristiano Ronaldo and Neymar all decide to forgo Barcelona, Real Madrid and Paris St. Germain for LA Galaxy, D.C United and Houston Dynamo.

What changed? What took the NASL from amateur teams playing in front of sparse crowds on terrible pitches to the envy of the soccer glitterati? One man, Steve Ross. He was the president of Warner Communications, a media mogul with fingers in music, cable television, video games and the comic book industry. He loved the Cosmos and was determined to make the club as success. He knew they needed something special, and there was nobody more famous than Pelé.

"I was retired from my team, Santos, I was retired from Brazil from the national team," Pelé told journalist Michael Lewis, the editor of BigAppleSoccer.com. "What I am going to do in New York? I come from the two biggest teams, the biggest moments. Clive Toye [New York Cosmos president] told me, 'Listen, we want to make soccer, football, as big as it is in Europe and South America.' When I signed with the Cosmos, the Cosmos were almost a university team. Later on, we became the best team, almost in the world. After we got some excellent players, then the Cosmos became No 1."

It all sounds so simple, but that's how the greats think. Pelé's three year, $2.8 million contract made him the best paid athlete in the world. His first game attracted television interest from over 200 countries and 300 journalists flew in to attend. He laid the path for the Cardiff-born Italian Giorgio Chinaglia to join the Cosmos from Lazio. This was a player in his prime, making the trip across the Atlantic to enhance his career, not finish it. Then came the German World Cup-winning captain Franz Beckenbauer and his Brazilian World Cup captain, Carlos Alberto.

Nightclubs and red-carpets begged for the Cosmos squad to attend glitzy events. They accepted. The club went on worldwide tours hand in hand with the Warner brand. The team won not because of tactics but pure technical superiority. And all this in a New York City that was a mess. President Ford had rejected the city's plea for a financial bailout to help combat a notorious crime rate. In the summer of 1977, .44 Caliber Killer 'Son of Sam' terrorized the city with random killings. Times Square was a seedy, filthy, dangerous place to be. Looting was rife. This was Batman's Gotham or the home of Alan Moore's *Watchmen*, not a city fit for a king. And yet Pelé was happy to tirelessly sign autographs for fans until team officials had to remind him of his schedule and drag him away. In June, 62,394 American souls piled into the Giants Stadium for a 3-0 victory against the Rowdies. Pelé, who would turn 38 in the fall, scored a hat-trick.

His retirement game was a glitzy evening witnessed by 75,646 people shoulder to shoulder inside the New York Giants' stadium. The celebrities in attendance included Robert Redford, Barbra Streisand, Diane Keaton, Mick Jagger, Muhammad Ali and Henry Kissinger. Jeff Carter, the son of then President Carter, presented Pelé with a plaque and read: "Presented to Pelé for the smiles he put on children's faces, the thrills he gave to fans of this nation and the dimension he added to American sports. Pelé has elevated the game of soccer to heights never before attained in America and only Pelé, with his status, incomparable talent and beloved compassion could have accomplished such a mission. The United States of America is deeply grateful."

Pelé took the microphone: "Ladies and gentlemen, I am very happy to be there with you in this greatest moment of my life," he said. "I want to thank you all every single one of you. I want to take this opportunity to ask you to pay attention to the young of the world, the children, the kids. We need them too much." Some tears appeared on Pelé's cheeks. He gathered himself, then said, "And I want to ask you because I think that - I believe that - love is more important than what we can take in life. Everything passes. Please say with me, three times – Love! Love! Love!"

Roberta Flack sang The Star Spangled Banner, then Sérgio Mendes and his band played the Brazilian national anthem. Meanwhile, the stadium scoreboard was re-programmed to repeat the words – "Love! Love! Love!" and the crowd responded in unison. What did it mean? Maybe everything, maybe nothing. But in the long run, no explanation, no mix of words or memories can touch that sense of knowing that the crowd had that day. That they were there, in the stadium in that corner of time, whatever it meant for American soccer.

10. THE BIRTH OF A NATION

"You're a child of God, you've got purpose."
~ NAT TURNER, *Birth of a Nation*

"Johan Cruyff painted the chapel. And Barcelona coaches since merely restore or improve it."
~ PEP GUARDIOLA

"Americans want and expect the best," wrote the great Dutchman Johan Cruyff in his autobiography. If Pelé would be remembered for teaching people to love soccer in the US, then it was Cruyff who encouraged them to read the game. Cruyff had been instrumental in Ajax's dominance of European soccer in the early 1970s, dragging the club from obscurity to the very pinnacle of the world stage. Most significantly, together with coach Rinus Michels, he invented 'Total Football', in which any outfield player was able to take over the role of any other player in the team. It was a bold ethos, but a system of harmony. The more you learn about Cruyff, the more he becomes the game's most important figure.

On the international stage, Cruyff led the Netherlands to a

runners-up medal in the 1974 World Cup. They knocked out Argentina, East Germany and Brazil, before meeting West Germany in the final. At the kick off, Cruyff passed the ball back to his team-mates, who kept possession for 15 passes before returning it to Cruyff, who drove up the pitch and won a penalty, slammed home by Johan Neeskens. West Germany fought back to win 2-1, but the World Cup is remembered for Holland's patterns and possession, driven and dictated by Cruyff.

In an interview published in *World Soccer* magazine, Carlos Alberto, the captain of the Brazilian team that won the 1970 World Cup, said, "The only team I've seen that did things differently was Holland at the 1974 World Cup in Germany. Since then everything looks more or less the same to me.... Their 'carousel' style of play was amazing to watch and marvellous for the game." It was a vision or order, properly executed, that led to grandiose comparisons with great artists and composers. The whole philosophy of how soccer could be played was adjusted during that tournament.

However the story of Cruyff's arrival in America reads more like farce. After moving to Barcelona from childhood club Ajax, Cruyff had delivered the Catalans their first La Liga title since 1960, and, according to a *New York Times* journalist, did more for the spirit of Catalonia in a 5-0 win against Real Madrid than many politicians had managed in years of struggle. In 1978 he was all set to retire, having refused to play in the 1978 World Cup. He feared for his family's safety after a kidnapping attempt had taken place at his home in Barcelona the previous fall.

Luckily - and profitably - for soccer, Cruyff's first move in retirement was to be conned into some bad investments, notably a pig farm, by a French-Russian chancer called Michel Basilevitch. This was an individual who Cruyff's own wife called, "the most handsome man in the world." Cruyff was a laughing stock. He lost most of his life savings and the family flat was repossessed. Luckily, at 31, there was enough juice in his legs to go back to work. "Sometimes you don't realise how foolish you're being until someone points out that you're deluding yourself," Cruyff later said. "Then you honestly have to admit your mistake. That you're not interested in pigs at all."

Ever since World War II, California had been strangely plagued by wild men on motorcycles. Now the hills surrounding the City of Angels would bear witness to a flying Dutchman. Cruyff entertained the idea of signing for the New York Cosmos, but joined the Los Angeles Aztecs instead because his mentor Rinus Michels was at the helm (and he hated the idea of playing on artificial grass). "We decided to restart our lives. America was where I discovered new ambitions and how to develop them," he said. "I found my place in a completely new world." Once the decision had been made, the negotiations were completed quickly, the twelve-hour flight from Spain was booked and Cruyff was on the field just four hours after landing. He scored twice in seven minutes, before providing an assist and leaving the pitch to a standing ovation.

Cruyff went on to score 13 goals in 23 games in th 1978-79 season, bagging the MVP honours. But when the Aztecs were then sold to Mexican investors who wanted to turn the club into a Latin enclave, that was that. Cruyff had signed a contract not with the Aztecs, but with the league itself, the NASL. Having spent years shoe-gazing on the edges of relevance, the Washington Diplomats and their newfound part-owners, Gulf & Western corporation, paid a million bucks to bring Cruyff to Washington, where Barbara Kennedy helped find him a house and his neighbour was Secretary of Defense, Robert McNamara. He bought a pair of Doberman Pinschers.

Despite his new entourage, Cruyff clashed continuously with British head coach Gordon Bradley, who was less 'Total Football' and more 'Win At All Costs'. Cruyff saw it as his job to organize the team, but the press in D.C. started panning him as a disappointment because he wasn't scoring goals. Ever the diplomat, Cruyff hit back:

"Forget about organization, I'm going to play spectacularly now," he told the Dips' beat writer, John Feinstein. "I'm going to play soccer for the spectator. We'll start winning games. But no championships. If you want to win trophies you have to play organized."

Cruyff played the whole 1980 campaign for the 'Dips', scoring 12 goals in 30 games, as well as laying on a slathering of assists. They shattered NASL attendance records and entered the play-offs, only to be dumped out by Cruyff's old coach Michels and the Aztecs. Gulf & Western pulled the rip chord, citing losses of $6 million. Cruyff returned to Spain with Levante, but America had lodged itself in his mind. The school sports system was something of a revelation to Cruyff, who knew nothing other than the club system in Europe. He admired the way the U.S. saw sport and school work as two sides of the same coin. "We split them up, they bring them together. In America, a real Einstein understands sport, and a real sportsman understand Einstein."

Cruyff's time in America made him question why sportsmen are lampooned in the European media as dim. He was correct, as usual. Passing judgment on soccer players talking in front of bright lights and a TV camera is a one-dimensional interpretation of intelligence, and Cruyff saw things in 3D. Intelligence is not determined exclusively by IQ, nor good scores in English or Math. Science has shown us instead that intelligence is multidimensional. Intelligence is the ability to accomplish complex goals over a sustained period of time. Intelligence is LeBron James analyzing new opponents and variants almost instantly, adding them to the database in his head and finding a way to the beat them, again and again and again. Intelligence is the confidence, brainpower and focus required to keep Cristiano Ronaldo firing on all cylinders and breaking Champions League records well into his mid-thirties. Cruyff understood soccer and soccer players in these terms, so had a much more nuanced view of how sport and society interact.

Cruyff understood intelligence and in America he came to understand politics. When your neighbour's the Secretary of State, soft skills rub off. He was often given the inside-line on the running of the Dips by general manager Andy Dolich. He learnt the mechanics of management, from cutthroat politics to grassroots philanthropy, and it prepared him for a spectacular managerial career. The trophies alone amounted to a European Cup, two European Cup Winners' Cups and four Spanish league titles. So as a player he had led them to their first league title in 14 years, and as a manager their first European Cup, but his real legacy remains a reinvention of modern soccer. He overhauled Barcelona's youth academy, *La Masia*, replacing the policy of selecting players with potential physique with those who "pampered the ball with their touch and pressed the opposition like rats." He made every team in the club, from the under-8s to Barça B, play the same 3-4-3, possession-based formation. Guardiola, Xavi, Iniesta, Pique, Messi all reaped the rewards.

"Even today I'm still a bit proud to have been one of those people, along with Pelé, Franz Beckenbauer, Johan Neeskens and all the rest, who pioneered the rise of soccer in that still developing continent," he wrote in retirement. "When I see how soccer is improving there, I know it's just a matter of time before an American team wins the World Cup. As a soccer lover, I'd think that was great." America couldn't have done it without Cruyff, but perhaps Cruyff wouldn't have gone on to achieve the rest - and launch a legacy that has touched all great teams since - without the United States of America.

11. MODERN TIMES

"Words are cheap. The biggest thing you can say is 'elephant'."
~ CHARLIE CHAPLIN, Modern Times

"Covfefe."
~ DONALD TRUMP

While we were enjoying ourselves at soccer's baby shower in *The Birth of a Nation*, tactical angles were being tinkered with on the European continent, but not for the better. Soccer players became fitter, defences became stingier, man-marking infiltrated coaches' thinking and the romantic aesthetic of a second striker dissolved into the pragmatism of playing a fifth midfielder. This wasn't innovation. It was risk-management. It was avoid-losing-at-all-costs, blighting the beauty and shackling the development of the game.

From Bill Gates, Steve Jobs and Larry Page, we know that explosive things can happen when someone comes at things from a different angle. Or, for that matter, with a different hat. When Kanye West, who is famous in part for saying "George Bush doesn't care about white people" in the wake of Hurricane Katrina, put on a Make America Great Again hat and held a pow-wow with Republican Trump, some saw his behaviour as hurtful and reckless. Some genuinely saw it as genius. It was completely unexpected. "We are both dragon energy," West wrote on Twitter. "He is my brother. I love everyone. I don't agree with everything anyone does. That's what makes us individuals. And we have the right to independent thought."

Luckily for soccer, a young Italian man, a former shoe salesman called Arrigo Sacchi, arrived on the scene in the 80s wielding independent thought. He held a proclivity to separate problems from solutions and the energy to drag soccer back from the brink. He had watched the Dutch side of the 1970s and had spent some years meditating on how the game should be played. He said, "It really took my breath away. It was a mystery to me. The television was too small; I felt like I need to see the whole pitch fully to understand what they were doing and fully to appreciate it."

As a teenager in his hometown of Fusigano on the river Senio in northeast Italy, Sacchi had also watched the great Hungarian side of Ferenc Puskás that shocked Wembley in *The Empire Strikes Back*. The flea-like energy he witnessed electrified a mind used to watching slow, methodical phases of play piped into his television set. He believed that soccer could change for the better, that a team could press in a 4-4-2 formation and that he could win the Scudetto even though he had never managed in *Serie A*. His single mindedness made his AC Milan side one of - perhaps the - greatest in modern soccer history.

Like Hogan and Meisl (*The Graduate*) and Chapman (*West Side Story*) before him, Sacchi was no great player. But this was no impediment to coaching. "I never realised that to become a jockey you needed to be a horse first," he told a crowd at Bocconi University in Milan who questioned his credentials. When Sacchi's *Serie B* Parma were drawn against AC Milan at the San Siro in the 86-87 Coppa Italia, the gusto of his team's pressing was already the talk of the Italian broadsheets.

"And we had several types of pressing that we would vary throughout the game," he later said. "There was partial pressing, where it was more about jockeying; there was total pressing, which was more about winning the ball; there was fake pressing, where we pretended to press, but, in fact, used the time to recuperate." Parma beat Milan 1-0 in the group stage and again in the first knockout round with the same scoreline. The billionaire media mogul owner of the *Rossonieri*, Silvio Berlusconi, hired him and bestowed three years to achieve success. He needed just one.

Like Cruyff, Sacchi believes in the power of the collective unit. A fountain of some of the greatest quotes in managerial history, he once said: "The only way you can build a side is by getting players who speak the same language and can play a team game. You can't achieve anything on your own, and if you do, it doesn't last long. I often quote what Michelangelo said: 'The spirit guides the hand.'" The squad he inherited in 1987 was made up of Italian greats Franco Baresi and Mauro Tassotti, future greats Paolo Maldini and Alessandro Costacurta, and the Dutchmen Ruud Gullit and Marco van Basten. They were later joined by fellow Dutch master Frank Rijkard, ironically after he had fallen out with Cruyff, who was back at Ajax as head coach.

His first miracle was getting stars from across Europe to unite behind his vision. His second was getting them to train without the ball. For

Sacchi, shape was everything, so he coined the term 'shadow play', in which players trained as a unit, maintaining their shape and adapting their press according to where Sacchi told them the imaginary ball was. Milan had won the title just once in the previous twenty years, and yet four years later, Sacchi had bagged a Scudetto, back-to-back European Cups and two Intercontinental Cups. The key to everything was the determination to squeeze the space between the lines to just twenty-five meters from the last defender to the center forward. Teams attempting to play through them had to break down three lines in quick succession, as well as navigate an aggressive offside trap. "And thus, the team had to move as a unit up and down the pitch, and also from left to right."

Before Real Madrid won back-to-back Champions Leagues in 2016 and 2017, Sacchi's AC Milan was the last club to claim Europe's top competition in consecutive years, with his 89-90 vintage being named as the best club side of all time by *World Soccer* magazine in 2006. Waking up in Barcelona the morning after Milan hammered Steaua Bucharest 4-0 in the 1989 European Cup final, Sacchi said that he had a feeling he had never experienced before. "It was one which I have never experienced since. I had this unusual, sweet taste in my mouth. I realised it was the apotheosis of my life's work."

Significantly, the *World Soccer* list included national teams too. Sacchi's Milan was fourth, and the first three were Hungary 1954, Brazil 1970 and Holland 1974. Furthermore, it's a side that remains frozen in time. In 2005, the offside law was changed again, to exclude any players who were technically offside but not actually 'interfering' with play. The result was that it was no longer possible to play Sacchi's double-bind of aggressive pressing and a high offside line. Sacchi wanted to play within half the length of an Olympic swimming pool, but today the game has been stretched to an average area of 55-60 meters.

Anyone browsing YouTube for highlights of the 1990 World Cup in Italy could easily misinterpret the powerful footage of opera legend Luciano Pavarotti belting out the tournament's theme music, *Nessun dorma* as representative of drama. *Nessun dorma* translates as 'none shall sleep', but Italia '90 was a tournament so dull (and the 1992 Euros that followed) that it led to FIFA changing the rules of the game. They prohibited goalkeepers from picking up a deliberate back pass, enforcing less time-wasting and more attacking, as well as outlawing the tackle from behind. FIFA has done much wrong, but here they did only right, changing the game forever for the better.

Sacchi stepped down as Milan manager in 1991 to take control of the Italian national team, and justifiably based much of his early team selections on his former side. His departure from club management coincided with the emergence of the Argentine Marco Biesla. There are people who consider themselves fans of European soccer who won't be able to tell you who Biesla is, but he links the tactical lineage between Michels, Cruyff, Sacchi and Guardiola. He may never be held in the same esteem as those great names who have hauled so much silver, but he stands among them as an inspiration, an innovator, and a bastion of soccer knowledge.

He grew up in an ambitious, career-driven family where the pursuit of knowledge and success were one and the same. But he was independent, refusing to support his father's team Rosario Central, opting instead for Newell's Old Boys, where Maradona had played at the end of his career. He refused, too, to study politics or law and tried instead to make it as a player, but it wasn't his destiny. He quit to study physical education and prepare to be a coach. He studied soccer routinely, obsessively, locking himself in his room to analyze videos and search for the innovation that could stamp his mark on the game.

Taking charge of his boyhood club Newell's Old Boys, he conceived a
4-3-3/3-4-3 system and a doctrine of four principles: *Concentración,
Permanente movilidad, Rotación y Repenitización* (Concentration,
Permanent focus, Rotation and Improvisation). You occasionally hear
something similar when reading about Silicon Valley luminaries,
who will quote *kaizen*, the Japanese word for continuous improve-
ment. He guided Newell's to the Copa Libertadores final in 1992,
where they lost to São Paulo, but his team was enough to earn him a
stint as Argentina coach, winning an Olympic gold in 2004, then on
to the top job with Chile, where he made *La Roja* one of the most
thrilling teams in world soccer in a 3-3-1-3 formation. They reached
the World Cup quarter finals in 2010, but were thwarted by Brazil. As
coach of Athletico Bilbao between 2009 and 2011, he dumped Sir Alex
Ferguson's Manchester United out of the Champions League. Pep
Guardiola has called him "the best coach in the world."

Bielsa represents the antithesis of the negative soccer that had flat-
tered to deceive fans before FIFA intervened. He is an aggressive,
romantic idealist, obsessive about attack and pushing ideas that can
safeguard the evolution of soccer. Writing about NFL, Chris Brown,
author of *The Art of Smart Football*, says: "There is no such thing as
Platonic ideal football; there is no right or wrong way to do things,
and the game is governed by a few simple things: the size and speed
of the players, the geometry of their arrangement on a football field,
and, above all else, pragmatism – what is good is simply what works."
Bielsa has his own take: "A man with new ideas is a madman, until
his ideas triumph."

12. THE GODFATHER

"The most important characters in mythology were Apollo and Dionysus. Apollo represented reason and Dionysus represented emotion. Those who knew Maradona understand that he was the worst of Apollo, but the best of Dionysus."
    ~ LUCIANO DE CRESCENZO, Italian Journalist

"A friend should always underestimate your virtues and an enemy overestimate your faults."
    ~ DON VITO CORLEONE, *The Godfather*

Ever since the German philosopher Karl Marx, there have been some who have viewed the world through a lens of suffering. If you're successful, you're an oppressor, and if you're not, it must be someone else's fault. Even before Marx, there were obviously ethnic and racial and gender differences that manifest themselves in prejudice, but the only bulletproof way to beat this - and perhaps the best idea that the world has ever had - is measuring the individual alongside their experience of culture.

This is dangerous territory, so I will preface my take on the debate by pointing out that players can only be products of their age. Making comparisons between decades is a largely arbitrary exercise. This is just a prediction, but if a player is to better Messi in our lifetimes, then they will surely be a product of a broader evolution in mankind, with reinforced knees, amplified cognition and general bioenhancement.

That said, there are only two players - Pelé and Maradona - that will show up in every single conversation about the greatest player ever. There are another three - Cruyff, Di Stefano and Puskás who show up in most. Then there's Zinedine Zidane, Messi, both Ronaldos and Franz Beckenbauer who are shoe-ins for the top ten. But fundamentally the debate is between Pelé and Maradona. Purely on paper, the accolade goes to Pelé, or to use his full name, Edson Arantes do Nascimento. He was involved in three World Cup wins (he played and scored in the 1958 and 1970 finals, but was injured in 1962), scored 1281 goals in 1363 games and is both the youngest winner of a World Cup - just 17 when he scored twice in the final - and one of only three players to have scored in four different World Cups. If we're taking a data-based approach, there's no room for debate. But we're not.

Maradona was - and remains - an outlaw. He has lived a life outside the law, beyond the law, not necessarily against it. The Argentinian coach Mauricio Pochettino tells a great story about sharing a room with Maradona as teammates at Newell's Old Boys in 1994. Maradona left the room they were sharing to go and watch a basketball final in Mar de Plata, but didn't come back to the hotel. "After breakfast we went to training. Nobody knew about Diego and at lunchtime it was breaking news on the television ... Diego shoots journalists in Buenos Aires! Four hundred kilometres away!"

His story began in poverty in a Buenos Aires slum, where his talented feet spirited him to debut for Argentinos Juniors at just 15. From there, he spent the next 20 years as the most colorful, flawed, brilliant, controversial player the game has ever seen. At Barcelona, he incited a mass brawl at the Spanish Cup final in front of the King of Spain. In Italy, he took Napoli, a club in the doldrums, to the very pinnacle of Italian soccer. He gave the fans silverware, pride and respect, breaking the dominance of the northern powerhouses of *Serie A* while servicing a cocaine habit the likes of which professional sport will never see again. When he left in 1991, the club retired its number 10 shirt. Back at Boca in 1997 after spells at Sevilla at Newell's Old Boys, he was able to rise to his last game - a 2-1 win in the *Superclasico* against eternal rivals River Plate - thanks to the coaching of disgraced Olympic sprinter Ben Johnson. But this was only after an intervention for failing another drugs test from the presidency of Ferrari-driving playboy Carlos Saul Menem. And that's only the half of it.

If Pelé's World Cup record reads like a straight-A student, then Maradona's is that of the classroom tearaway. He made his international debut for Argentina at 16, but a year later was controversially left out of the squad for the 1978 World Cup on home soil by César Luis Menotti, who thought he was too young. Four years later in Spain, he was shamefully sent off against arch-rivals Brazil as Argentina crashed out of the tournament in the second round. In 1986, he dominated the tournament, playing every minute of every game, captaining Argentina to victory in the final in Mexico City against West Germany. His two goals in the quarter final win against England are two of the most famous ever scored. The first, illegitimate, has come to be known as the 'Hand of God'. The second, four minutes later and legitimate, was voted 'Goal of the Century'. Defending the title in Italy in 1990, Maradona carried an ankle injury all the way to the final in Rome, where Argentina lost 1-0 to West Germany. In the United States in 1994, 17 years after his debut,

Maradona scored a sumptuous first-round goal against Greece in Boston, before being kicked out of the tournament, disgraced, for failing a drugs test.

For Cruyff, soccer was not a game but an emotion, and it's possible to see this in the eyes of the Argentine. Maradona mainlined soccer until the well ran dry and his body crumbled. But when you have come from poverty and delivered a World Cup, there is little the people will not forgive. So instead of succumbing to shame, he became a deity. "Genius round the world stands hand in hand, and one shock of recognition runs the whole circle round." Herman Melville said that in the winter of 1850, delivering consensual truth to a complex matter. To live the life of Diego would be to experience a genius dancing with demons and living to tell the tale, like falling down an elevator shaft and landing in a pool of mermaids.

13. THE SEARCHERS

"A human rides a horse until it dies, then he goes on afoot. A Comanche comes along, gets that horse up, rides him 20 more miles... and then he eats him."

    ~ ETHAN, *The Searchers*

"The secret is to believe in your dreams; in your potential that you can be like your star, keep searching, keep believing and don't lose faith in yourself."

    ~ NEYMAR

History is hard to know. Cruyff once said, "Everything I have done has been with a view to the future, concentrating on progress, which means that the past is not something I think too much about." And yet looking into soccer's past has shown us that the rhythms that have dictated development can be distilled into two distinct elixirs: speed and imagination.

At Barcelona between 2008 and 2012, Guardiola built his mesmeric 'tiki-taka' team (a phrase the coach himself dislikes) and fans around the world were convinced soccer had reached its apex. And yet a year after Guardiola departed for a sabbatical in New York, Bayern Munich put Barcelona to the sword in the 2012-2013 Champions League semi-final with a 7-0 drubbing over two legs. They matched Barcelona's passing and pressing, but they did it with bigger, hungrier players. So to speed and imagination, we can add strength, just as a US audience, experiencing a difficult time with worries over brain injuries for children and adults playing American football, comes online. In April 2014, an article in the *New York Times* called soccer "a conversation topic you can no longer ignore." The truth was in the television, where 30 million viewers had tuned in for Premier League matches screened on NBC Universal, averaging 440,000 viewers each.

I promised that this book would take no longer to read than to watch a game on the television, so the clock is ticking down and it is time to end, as it were, at the beginning. Once, I was asked to explain the appeal of soccer to somebody. A somebody whose intelligence was big and piercing and made me feel like I was stuck inside high walls of black glass. I started talking.

It went something like this:

"What you see when you read headlines about an arrogant, woman-ising or racist millionaire is someone who's famous because he's good at kicking a ball. But the reality for anyone who's grown up playing soccer is that isn't what they see. Instead, they see someone who's unbelievably good at what they do. To start with, they're an elite athlete. They're also exceptionally talented. But more than that, they've worked immensely hard to get where they are. Depending on their background, they've either made huge sacrifices or taken enormous risks, battling to make it in what might even be the most competitive job industry there is. So when you see a game of soccer on the telly, that's 22 of these super-humans going at each other with a combined sum of experience, athleticism and artistry that you can only appreciate because you weren't nearly good enough to compete with them yourself. Then, on top of that, forget *The X-Factor*, this is the greatest soap opera on earth. The characters, the politics, the money, the story arcs, the tragedy, the glory. It's unbelievable entertainment."

I realised as I arrived at my smug crescendo that this was more or less nonsense. Truthfully, I couldn't tell him. I just knew that I knew and that somehow or other I was going to have to squeeze it out of myself. I was going to have to sit there and self-induce. But hey, so it goes. Soccer does this to people. It has been doing this to people while wars have been fought and dictators overthrown. But soccer's more important than a lot of people give it credit for. It is impossible, for example, to understand the breakup of Yugoslavia without realising the role played by soccer is elevating a nation's perception of itself.

Except I'm not here to talk about tribes or politics or anything that's familiar to the initiated. Aristotle said that "the initiated do not learn anything but they suffer and feel, experience impressions and moods." If I can consider anyone who's read this far to be initiated, then that saves me some headspace for the tricky part.

In 1999, the American author Joe McGinniss published *The Miracle of Castel di Sangro*, a true story about a village soccer team living a bold season in the second-highest professional league in Italy.

There's a quote inside the front cover:

"Years have gone by and I've finally learned to accept myself for who I am: a beggar for good soccer. I go about the world, hand outstretched, and in the stadiums I plead: 'A pretty move, for the love of God.' And when good football happens, I give thanks for the miracle and don't give a damn which country or team performs it."

They're the words of the legendary Uruguayan writer Eduardo Galeano. They capture a dialogue about soccer which is far more significant than the one played out in the media every week. It reaches into what makes soccer so magnetic, the thing that's too often brushed aside by the powers more interested in fuelling the money and militarism of a global phenomenon. Soccer, it turns out, is much more than we are told it is.

If a book is a souvenir of an idea, then good soccer occupies that same cathartic space. That dream you had last night, or the music or the cinema, they're all real. When the image and the story and the setting and the noise align and become real in you, everything swells to a crescendo, for which soccer has the ultimate point of detonation: A goal. Ecstasy. And if those preceding moments include good soccer, as Galeano spent a life yearning for, then you can be excused for collapsing in awe.

I collapsed in awe once. The 2006 World Cup semi-final between Italy and Germany is the greatest game of soccer I've ever seen. It rocked and swelled with a breathtaking sense of destiny. You knew at 0-0 in extra time that whoever won that game would win the World Cup. It took 119 minutes, but then Italian playmaker Andrea Pirlo, playing for MLS side New York City at the time of writing, slipped a delicately disguised pass inside the box to full back Fabio Grosso, who stroked home from the right with his left foot. Grosso's face was full of disbelief as he was mobbed by teammates and the Italian crowd in Dortmund opened their hearts to victory. In the seconds that were left of the game, Alessandro del Piero found everything in his lungs to latch onto a no-look pass from fellow substitute Alberto Gilardino and gracefully chip the ball into the roof of the net.

I wanted to commune with those moments. They represented everything that soccer could and should inspire, with the crowd's flashbulbs pulsing like warning lights, imagining utopia, catastrophe and everything in between.

$\sim$

The End

14: BONUS CHAPTER: THE BEST SOCCER FORMATIONS

What's the best soccer formation? Patience, young Padawan, for you have much to learn. If there were one single best soccer formation, the world would surely stop turning. We wouldn't see so many variations and experimentations, births, deaths and re-births. In short, evolution itself would end.

A long time ago (*Creation*), in the first international game between Scotland and England at Partick, England lined up in a 1-2-7, Scotland a 2-2-6. How times have changed.

Since then, coaches have played an elaborate game of cat and mouse, striving for numerical advantage in decisive areas of the pitch, looking for clever ways to exploit space and opposition weaknesses and get the most out of the specific attributes of their best players.

As far as more recent trends go, I present a selection of formations that have been stress-tested at most levels of soccer. Before we start, the key thing to remember is that your players are indivisible from your formation (unless you're playing 5-a-side). So your task is not to find a template that you like the tactical or philosophical look of and then crowbar you players into that shape. Instead, it's about organizing the players you have into a formation that gets the best out of them AND weakens the opposition.

When, for example, a 4-4-2 lines up against a 4-3-3, you can expect the 4-3-3- to have more possession because they have an extra midfielder, but the flipside is that they will be more vulnerable to attacks from wide areas. Therefore the team playing 4-4-2 needs to have fast, dangerous players out wide, or they're going to struggle. It's important to know that it's as much about what happens when you don't have the ball as when you do. In presenting to you the best soccer formations, the main thread will be which best suit which player attributes. It's the only place to start your decision.

4-4-2 FORMATION

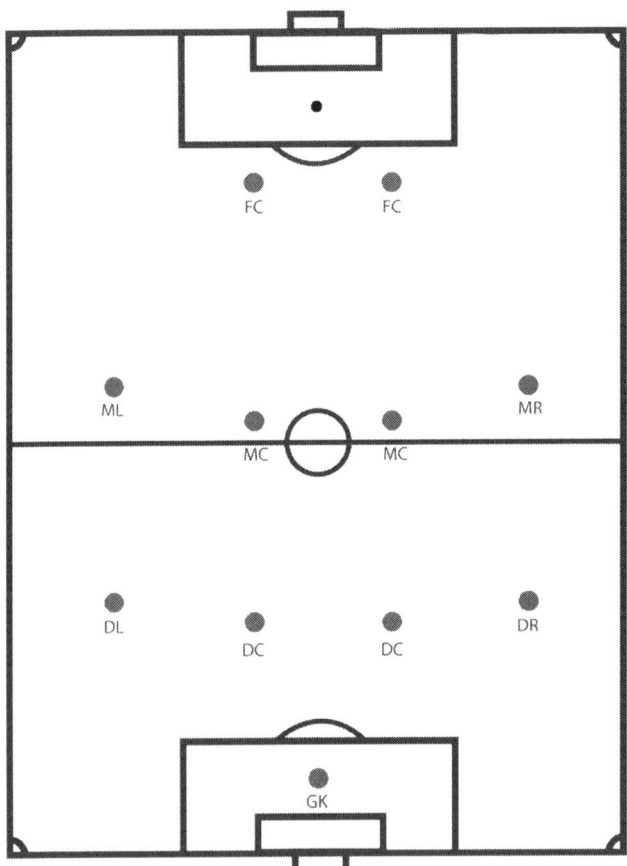

The Big Daddy of soccer formations. The Grand Master Default. The Go To. It's simple, easy to understand and execute, particularly at youth level, either as a 'flat four' midfield or a 'diamond', pairing a defensive-minded destroyer with a more attacking-minded player in behind the strikers. A diamond can also be described as 4-1-2-1-2.

This is a great choice when you've got players who can play in wide positions and make the pitch big. It suits good crossers of the ball, taking advantage of the wider gaps generated in the opposition's defensive line. And on a very simple level, it's arguably easier to score with two strikers than with one.

You'll need two central midfielders who are extremely fit and capable of attacking as well as defending. You'll also need to be wary when coming up against teams playing a three-man central midfield. When this happens, one of your strikers will need to be prepared to drop back into midfield and help out.

For some historical context, in the 1998-1999 season, Manchester United won the Premier League, FA Cup and Champions League playing a 4-4-2. However their 2-3 defeat to Real Madrid – who lined up in a 4-2-3-1 – at Old Trafford the following season persuaded Sir Alex Ferguson that the formation had had its day in elite European competition.

4-3-3 FORMATION

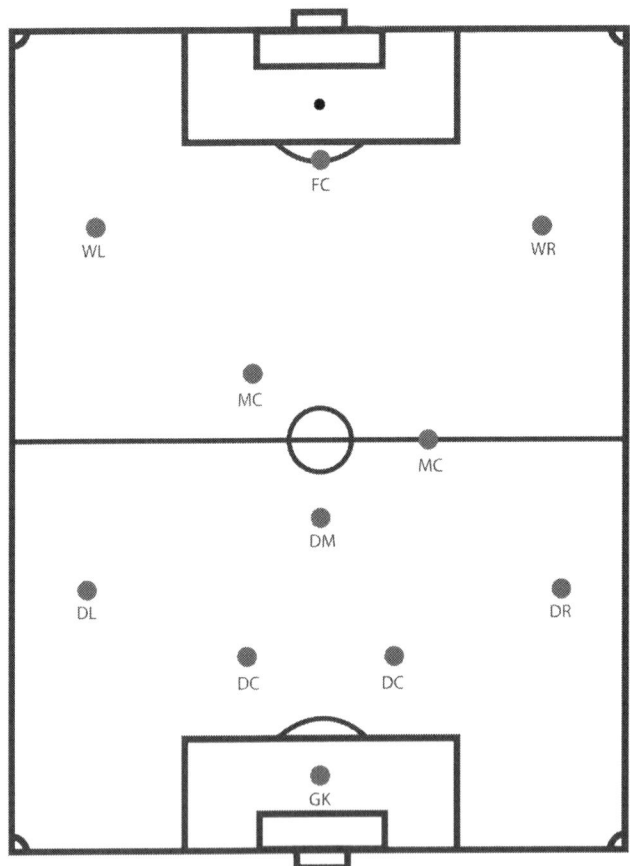

In one of my favourite comedian-meets-megastar videos, British funny man Lloyd Griffith tells Lionel Messi that he intends to use a 4-4-2 formation in his FIFA 16 Team of the Year. Messi smirks, and tells Griffith that what he really means is 4-3-3. This formation wants control of the midfield and fluidity in attack.

In a 4-3-3, by stretching or shrinking the distance between players, teams strive to make the pitch as big as possible when in possession of the ball, and as small as possible when not. The wingers need to have pace and shooting ability, while the FC can be either a powerful target man, or a 'False 9' like Messi, who drops deeper in the pitch to generate space for the wingers to exploit.

Sometimes, the roles of the central midfielders are assigned as destroyer, passer and creator. The best example of this is Pep Guardiola's Barcelona team in the 2008-2009 season. Sergio Busquets the Creator, Xavi Hernández the Passer and Andrés Iniesta the Creator.

This is the formation of Luis Enrique's Barcelona, but it can also be employed by amateur sides, providing they have good fitness. The problem with this formation is that teams who aren't good at keeping possession are vulnerable to counter attacks.

Use against: 4-4-2

4-2-3-1 FORMATION

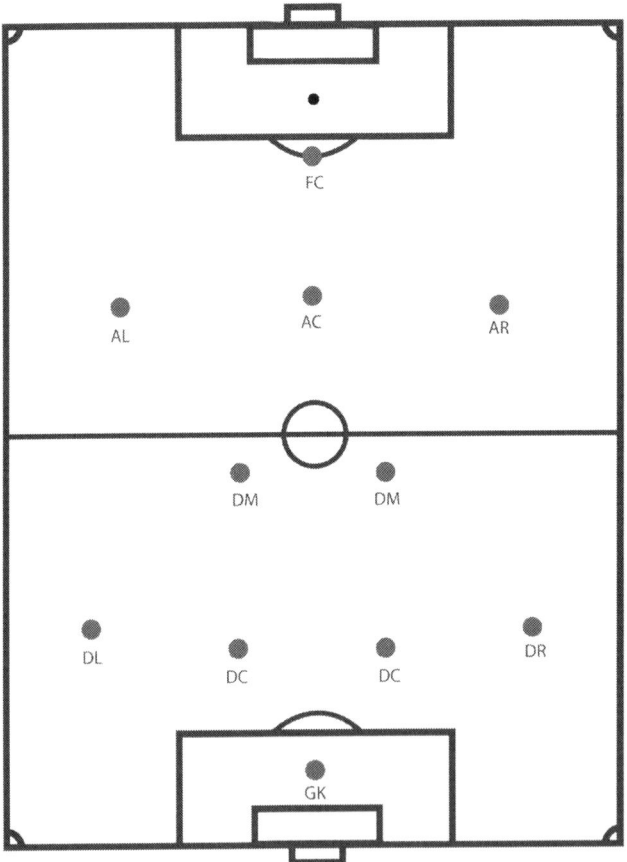

The first difference to point out is that unlike 4-4-2 and 4-3-2, a 4-2-3-1 has four rows of players, rather than three. A 4-2-3-1 allows teams to absorb pressure comfortable and then launch forward aggressively. It's got balance and flexibility.

The defensive unit, which is made up of two Centre Backs (DC) and two Defensive Midfielders (DM)s, is often referred to as the 'double pivot'. Once the ball is won thanks to the double pivot, the full backs (DL and DR) can bomb down the wings and know that they are covered by the DMs. They'll often look to cut inside and combine with the No. 10 Attacking Midfielder (AC), nominally the most creative player on the team who is comfortable both dribbling and passing quickly.

The 4-2-3-1 comes unstuck when the opposition full backs push high up the pitch, pinning the wingers back into their own half and rendering the formation a 4-5-1 with an isolated striker. You also need to make sure your wingers track back. If they don't, opposition wide players can easily overload your defence.

You'll notice that in the Barcelona of Messi, Suarez and Neymar, the Catalans had three players who can beat a defender on their own.

Use against: 4-4-2

3-5-2 FORMATION

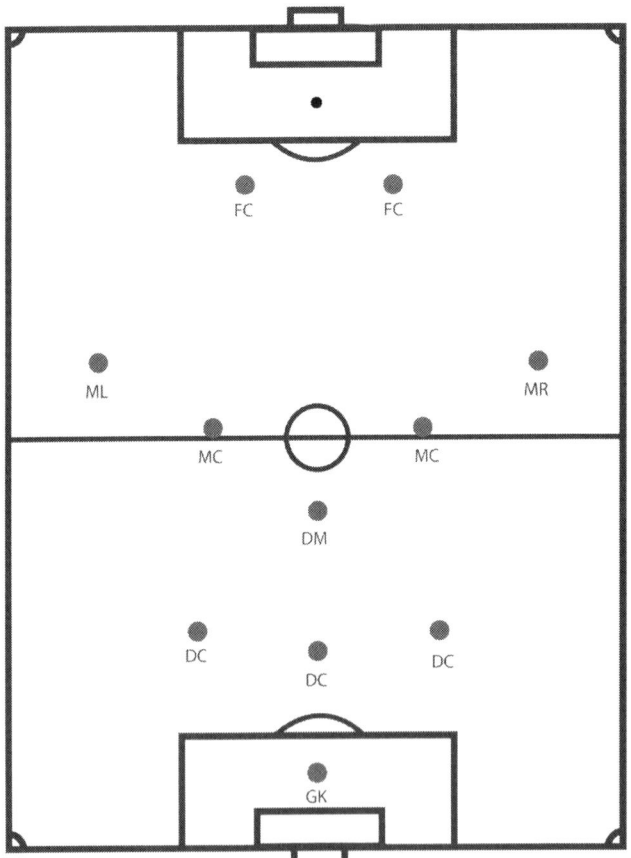

If you're worried that your defence is weak and you've got two players in your team who can run all day long, a 3-5-2 might work for you. Your wide men need to be comfortable with 50m sprints over and over again, effectively operating as wide defenders, midfielders and forwards.

With the option to quickly switch from a more defensive 5-3-2 to the attacking version 3-5-2 when you gain possession, you will almost always have a numerical advantage in midfield, especially when you're playing against 4-4-2.

Culturally, this is a formation favored by the Italians, who pride themselves on defensive excellence. The DM at the base of the midfield tends to sit quite deep. This is because any adventurous runs from the ML or MR will need cover. The formation also lends itself, when necessary, to the long forward ball to the two FCs.

Having five men in midfield is excellent if you're playing a side that likes to play on the counter attack, but generally this is a complex formation that requires more mental than physical resilience. Players are constantly having to cover for teammates and one of your DCs needs to be a very competent passer indeed.

Use against: 4-5-1

4-5-1 FORMATION

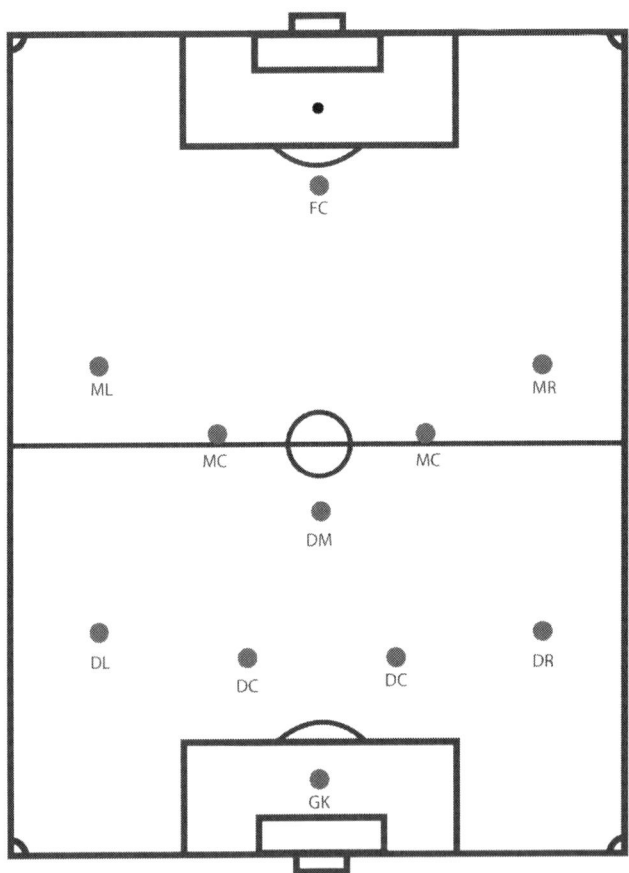

This is a very defensive formation. Packing the midfield can give you lots of possession and makes it difficult for the opposition to play through you. You'll often see this formation from teams in cup competitions who want to take the game to extra time or penalties. If the striker drops into midfield, you'll have yourself a 4-6-0.

The defenders are there to defend and nothing else, while two of the midfielders can organize themselves to form the double pivot you'll recognise from a 4-2-3-1. Alternatively, you can play with one holding midfielder whose sole purpose is to break up play. With the opportunity for quick, direct balls forward, the 4-5-1 lends itself well to hitting teams on the counter attack.

Going forward, you've got the two wide men and the lone striker. If he's quick, then it's about winning the ball ball in the middle and playing him through. If he's not, the rest of the formation needs to move up the pitch to offer him support.

Punters often point out that teams playing 4-3-3 will revert to a 4-5-1 when they're in the lead and want to close the game out. This is achieved with your two wingers playing a bit deeper.

Use against: 4-3-3

At the time of writing, this is soccer's most fashionable formation. It's also one of the most elusive, with variations of the basic structure revealing themselves as 5-2-3s or even 5-4-1s, depending on attacking and defensive transitions.

Followers of the EPL may be familiar with Eden Hazard's change in fortunes at Chelsea under Italian manager Antonio Conte. Freed from the defensive shackles of playing in a classic 4-2-3-1, Hazard flourished in a free-roaming attacking position on the left. Chelsea bought the Spanish specialist wing back Marcos Alonso from

Fiorentina, one suspects, for just this purpose and with dramatic results.

Playing three at the back means two proactive outside DCs either side of a spare man who's there to mop up any residual mess. The pair on the outside (at Chelsea, this is Cesar Azpilicueta and Gary Cahill) will track and scrap and even come into midfield to intercept. The middle man, a role currently played by the Brazilian David Luiz, will block, challenge for headers and make clearances.

Playing a three-man defence against a front three is a brave tactic however, especially when the opposition forwards are quick, confident players. Also, against a team that plays one up front, an extra spare man at the back runs the risk of being overmanned in midfield.

Don't use against: 4-5-1

3-4-2-1 FORMATION

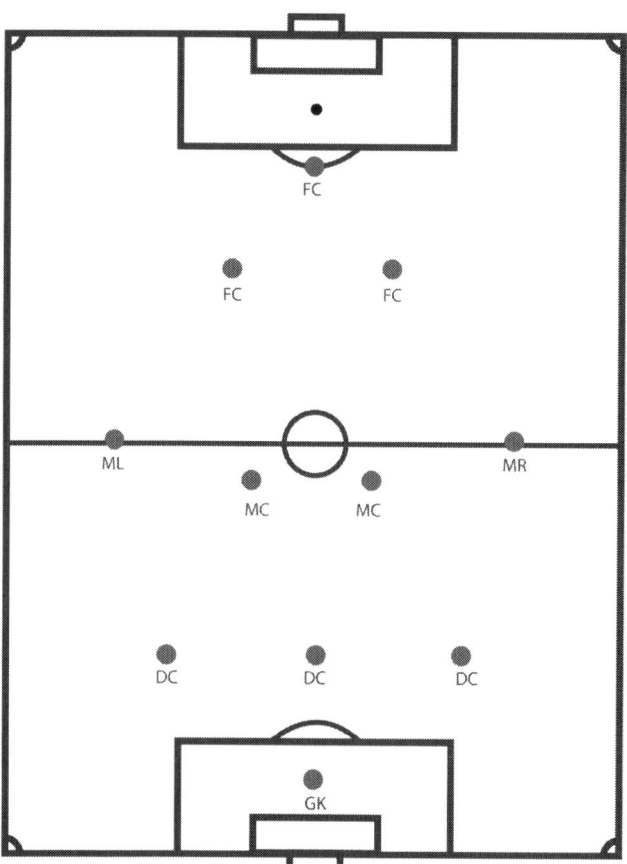

I'm biased here. It's the formation my team uses, having switched from the 4-3-3 we used last season. The switch came mainly because we were conceding too many goals. It was also to do with the emergence of an incredibly strong, but not especially mobile CF. Our most dangerous players are attacking midfielders, so this formation allows them to play off the FC and spend their time and energy closer to the goal.

The defense is built on two wide DCs and a central defensive anchor. Then there's a midfield line of four, followed by three attacking players who need to stay very close together. If you consider that the anchor plays a little deeper than his flanking CBs and that the FBs can push ahead of the two CMs, this effectively gives any team that plays this formation seven – yes, seven – passing lines (including the goalkeeper).

So it's a formation that suits a team that likes to keep the ball and move up the pitch together as a unit. It favors patience over pace and positioning over pressing. Our gameplan generally rests on forcing the opposition to move the ball to the wing backs, luring the wing back into playing down the line and then cutting off all options when the winger is forced to play the ball infield. The plan basically breaks down if the CF and AMs are lazy and let the opposition shift the ball across the back. You have been warned.

Use against: 4-2-3-1

5-2-3 / 5-4-1

As a recent tactical development, this concludes the soccer formation catalogue. This hybrid formation was conceived by Werder Bremen in Germany as a means to counteract the the false full back and reverse pyramid attacking shapes conceived by Pep Guardiola at Bayern Munich. It was later adopted by other Bundesliga teams and Juventus in the Champions League. With five defenders at the back, it's very difficult to stretch a team further across the pitch and open up gaps. It's incredibly flexible, because, as the brilliant Hungarian analyst István Beregi has pointed out, even if one of the full backs (DL or DR) moves up to press, there are still four defenders at the back, so defensive integrity is maintained. Ironically, despite its emergence as a countermeasure at the very highest level of the game, 5-2-3 / 5-4-1 can be employed successfully at youth level. From the goalkeeper, players can be instructed to always play short and move the ball out to the wings, encouraging possession, an appreciation of width and the opportunity to move up the pitch together.

Use against: Pep Guardiola

Soccer Formation Philosophy

A philosophical endnote. When Sacchi was briefly appointed Real Madrid's Sporting Director in 2004, he bemoaned a shift to reactionary soccer. He didn't like that because Zinedine Zidane, Raúl and Luis Figo didn't track back, it was necessary to put Claude Makélélé in as a ball winner in front of the back four.

"That's reactionary football. It doesn't multiply the players' qualities exponentially. Which, actually, is the point of tactics: to achieve this multiplier effect on the players' abilities. In my football, the *regista* – the playmaker – is whoever had the ball. But if you have [Claude]Makélélé, he can't do that. He doesn't have the ideas to do it, though of course, he's great at winning the ball. It's all about specialists." For Sacchi, this collective precision was paramount. It was about the universality of the system, where the greatness was about the sum of its parts and not the individual strengths of the players.

To make a modern comparison, the first meeting between Carlo Ancelotti's Bayern Munich and Thomas Tuchel's Dortmund was described by tactics expert Michael Cox:

"Ancelotti played a lopsided system designed entirely to get his best players in their favored positions, a formation which arguably lacked balance. Tuchel, on the other hand, played a system with key players out of position to suit the tactical demands of the game. Ancelotti is players-first, Tuchel is system-first."

What's more important to you?

REFERENCES

Books

- *Andrea Pirlo: I Think Therefore I Play*, by Andrea Pirlo
- *Arsene Wenger: The Biography*, by Xavier Rivoire
- *Barca: A People's Passion,* by Jimmy Burns
- *Barca: The Making of the Greatest Team in the World*, by Graham Hunter
- *Brilliant Orange: The Neurotic Genius of Dutch Football,* by David Winner
- *Cantona: The Rebel Who Would Be King*, by Philippe Auclair
- *From Cloisters to Cup Finals: A History of Charterhouse Football*, by Malcolm Bailey
- *Herbert Chapman, Football Emperor: A Study in the Origins of Modern Soccer*, by Stephen Studd
- *Inverting the Pyramid,* by Jonathan Wilson
- *Managing My Life: The Autobiography*, by Sir Alex Ferguson
- *Messi*, by Guillem Balague
- *Morbo: The Story of Spanish Football*, by Phil Ball
- *Mourinho: Anatomy of a Winner*, by Patrick Barclay

- *My Turn*, by Johan Cruyff
- *Pep Guardiola: The Evolution*, by Marti Perarnau
- *Pep Guardiola: Another Way of Winning: The Biography*, by Guillem Balague
- *Soccer in Sun and Shadow*, by Eduardo Galeano
- *The Ball is Round: A Global History of Soccer,* by David Goldblatt
- *The Life and Times of Herbert Chapman: The Story of One of Football's Most Influential Figures*, by Patrick Barclay
- *The Miracle of Castel di Sangro*, by Joe McGinniss
- *The Real Arsenal: From Chapman to Wenger*, by Brian Glanville
- *The Rebirth of Professional Soccer in America: The Strange Days of the United Soccer Association,* by Dennis J. Seese

Websites

- Si.com
- Wsc.co.uk
- Espn.com
- Nytimes.com
- 8by8mag.com
- Grantland.com
- Edition.cnn.com
- Worldsoccer.com
- Theguardian.com
- Fourfourtwo.com
- Calciomercato.com
- Bleacherreport.com
- Smithsonianmag.com
- Thesefootballtimes.co

www.pspfrench.com

ABOUT THE AUTHOR

Paul French was born in England and attended Charterhouse School, where the history books say that soccer was first played as long ago as 1862. After graduating from university, he played six seasons for the Old Carthusians, who won the FA Cup in 1881. He currently lives in Berlin and plays for the world-famous SFC Friedrichshain Internazionale, an international team which promotes acceptance and vocally opposes homophobia and sexism in soccer.

More from Paul French

Soccer Superpowers: Secrets In Fitness, Nutrition, Psychology, Tactics & Technique

A SINCERE REQUEST

If you liked this book and it helped you to develop a better understanding of soccer, then I need your help. In order for this book to
reach as many people as possible, it would be tremendous if you
could take a moment to leave an honest review on Amazon. The
more reviews it gets, the more people can learn about the beautiful
game.

Thank you!

GO VIP

To keep people up to date with future books, I am going to use a very special VIP email list, limited to the first 1000 people. If you're reading this in 2018, there's a good chance you'll get on the list.

As a VIP, you'll get a free, advanced copy of every book I ever write, forever. Thank you so much for reading, and lots more coming soon.

Get on the list by visiting this link...

http://eepurl.com/k632z

Printed in Poland
by Amazon Fulfillment
Poland Sp. z o.o., Wrocław